cake decorating skills

cake decorating skills

TRACEY MANN

FIREFLY BOOKS

A Firefly Book

Published by Firefly Books Ltd. 2011

Copyright © 2011 Quarto Inc.

First printing

Publisher Cataloging-in-Publication Data (U.S.)
Mann, Tracey, 1971–
    Cake decorating skills : techniques for every cake maker and every kind of cake / Tracey Mann
[176] p. : ill., col. photos. ;   cm.
Includes index.
Summary: A step-by-step guide to basic cake decorating skills and techniques, including covering a cake, and applying piping and embellishments.
ISBN-13: 978-1-55407-907-0 (pbk.)
1. Cake decorating. I. Title.
641.8/6539 dc22   TX771.2.M366   2011

Library and Archives Canada Cataloguing in Publication
Mann, Tracey, 1971-
    Cake decorating skills : techniques for every cake maker and every kind of cake / Tracey Mann
Includes index.
ISBN-13: 978-1-55407-907-0
1. Cake decorating. I. Title.
TX771.2.M36 2011   641.8'6539   C2011-900751-7

Published in the United States
by Firefly Books (U.S.) Inc.
P.O. Box 1338, Ellicott Station
Buffalo, New York 14205

Published in Canada
by Firefly Books Ltd.
66 Leek Crescent
Richmond Hill, Ontario L4B 1H1

Conceived, designed and produced by
Quarto Publishing plc
The Old Brewery, 6 Blundell Street
London N7 9BH
QUAR.CDSK

For Quarto:
Project Editor Lily de Gatacre
Copyeditor Liz Jones
Proofreader Sally MacEachern
Art Editor Joanna Bettles
Designer Lisa Tai
Illustrator Kuo Kang Chen
Art Director Caroline Guest
Photographer Philip Wilkins
Creative Director Moira Clinch
Publisher Paul Carslake

Colour separation in Singapore by
    Pica Digital Pte Ltd
Printed in Singapore by Star Standard

Contents

Foreword

If you've ever thought that cake decorating might be for you, let me take this opportunity to show you what a wonderful and creative activity it can be. I am a self-taught cake decorator. I've been running my cake business and teaching for over 18 years, and I'm delighted to now be able to pass on my accumulated knowledge to others who are just beginning to discover this inspiring and exciting pastime. In this book I aim to cover the basic and fundamental roots of cake decorating, showing simple yet effective ways of decorating cakes with confidence. I hope you enjoy using this book to create stunning cakes and, most importantly, have fun doing so!

Tracey Mann

CHAPTER 1

Getting started

Before you begin to discover the captivating art of sugar-craft, you will need a few essential pieces of equipment. Here you can see what tools are available and how they are used in different aspects of cake decorating, as well as get some great tips on designing your cakes.

Basic cake decorating equipment

There are some pieces of equipment that you will find invaluable as you begin cake decorating. Whatever the complexity of your design or other tools you use, these essentials will prove to be highly useful.

Nonstick rolling pin and board
These two tools are indispensable for rolling fondant, gum paste or chocolate paste for covering cakes and creating decorations.

Cake pans
The first decision to make is what size and shape your cake will be. There is a huge selection available.

Turntable
Putting a cake on a turntable can help you see more clearly when decorating. Tilted ones offer a better view.

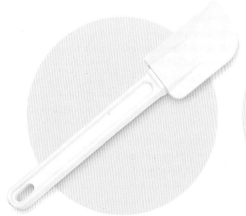

Spatula
This is necessary for effectively mixing your icing, especially when working with buttercream.

Toothpicks
These little sticks are incredibly useful for many things, such as adding paste colors to icing and supporting models.

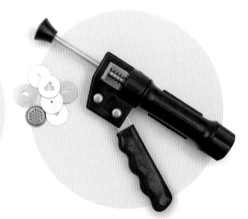

Sugar-craft gun
With a variety of attachments available, a sugar-craft gun is a great tool for extruding icing to create a huge array of effects.

Scissors
From cutting ribbons to removing excess fondant when modeling, a good, sharp pair of scissors is an invaluable tool.

Tape measure
Use this to measure cakes and cake boards to make covering and stacking cakes easier for a polished and stable result.

Parchment paper or waxed paper
From making piping bags to creating templates and aiding with delicate piping work, these basics are must-haves.

Paintbrushes
Apart from painting on sugar colors, paintbrushes are also useful for removing any excess icing or dust from your designs.

Mixing bowls
You will need a good selection of glass and plastic bowls in various sizes. Bowls with lids are useful for storing batches of icing.

Further tools and equipment
There is a huge range of cake decorating tools available to help you achieve better results and more ambitious cakes. Specific tools relating to each area of cake decorating are listed at the start of each section in this book. Play around with the tools as you just might discover a new effect or time-saving measure.

Designing cakes

Designing cakes is an exciting challenge and a chance to practice the skills you will learn from this book. Be careful not to overcomplicate your cakes though — trying to use every skill on one cake will make the cake look really busy! Simple cake designs can often be the most attractive.

Design considerations

Each cake design starts with gathering some basic information. Ask yourself the following questions:

- Who is the cake for? Man, woman, child?
- What is the celebration? Birthday, anniversary, wedding?
- How many people is the cake for? (See page 168 for advice on quantities.)
- What type of cake would the recipient like? Sponge cake, chocolate cake, fruit cake?
- What type of covering? Chocolate, fondant, buttercream?
- What is the recipient's favorite color?
- What would the recipient like on their cake? Would they like it to be a straightforward square birthday cake or a novelty shape?
- Is there any further information? A message for the cake? Hobbies, interests, anything that makes the cake personalized?

These are all very important questions, and once you have gathered this information you can start to plan, working with the skills you feel confident in. Sketch out your design before you start to create your cake. Don't commit to a design that you feel unsure about; be confident in what you are going to create. The best piece of advice in terms of cake design if you are starting out might be, "If you make a mistake, stick a rose on it." Maybe not literally and in all cases, but when you start covering cakes for the first time, don't

Polished product
Consider the size, shape, flavor, color and style of your cake before you start, and you can come up with stunning designs.

Avoiding waste
There is much less waste if a cake is cut in slices as illustrated below, rather than in wedges.

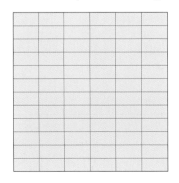 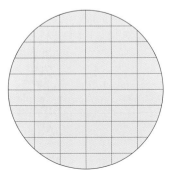

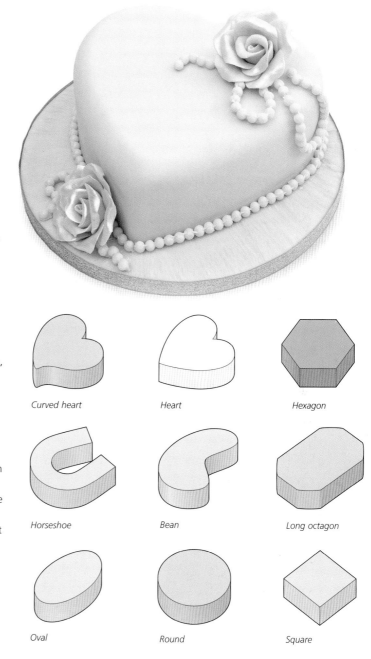

worry if the covering isn't as perfect as you want it to be. Look at your cake and decide which is the "best side" and keep that facing front. Lettering, flowers, stars and other shapes can easily be placed on areas you wish to cover by adapting your design slightly. Finally, be proud of what you have created!

Cake shapes

There are many differently shaped cake pans available, and the decision comes down to personal taste. Lots of people, when asked, will opt for a square cake because they imagine it is easier to cut. However, if you are a beginner, choose round cakes, as these are easier to cover than square ones. Square cakes can also look rather solid in tiered form. Avoid more complex shapes, such as petals and numbers, to begin with. If an ornate side decoration or floral display is required, it is often best to keep the shape of the cake fairly simple — round, oval, bean, curved leaf, scalloped oval, long octagonal, heart and curved heart shapes tend to be the easiest to work with and are fairly straightforward to ice. Petal shapes, hexagons and horseshoe-shaped cakes can be more difficult to work with — some caution and thought is needed before you agree to use these shapes in your final design. Don't promise someone a design that you will later regret!

Curved heart *Heart* *Hexagon*

Horseshoe *Bean* *Long octagon*

Oval *Round* *Square*

Many choices
An unusual shape can add excitement to a simply designed cake.

Cake tiers

Options for adding tiers include using a metal cake stand that will support the tiers separately with no pressure on the cakes or having the cakes stacked on top of each other (see pages 42–43). Pillars give a very traditional look to a wedding cake. There are also many different cupcake stands available, ranging from colored ones to clear acrylic. Think about the color scheme of your celebration before deciding which cake stand you want to use.

Cupcake stands

Don't be tempted to overload a cupcake stand, as it will look crowded. Leave some space, as shown on this mirrored stand.

Proportions and guidelines

There are traditional guidelines for the creation of tiered cakes. However, as fashions change, often the best guide is your eye and instinct. You may nonetheless find the following guidelines useful:

- Tiered wedding cakes normally have 2 or 3 inches (5 or 7.5 cm) between tier sizes. For example, a three-tier cake could have tiers of 6 inches (15 cm), 8 inches (20 cm) and 10 inches (25 cm), or 6 inches (15 cm), 9 inches (23 cm) and 12 inches (30 cm). The 3-inch (7.5 cm) gap allows more space for adding decorations, such as flower sprays.
- The top tier on a wedding cake tends to be no larger than 7 inches (18 cm). If the top tier is too large, the delicate triangle shape can be lost.
- Cakes that are going to be separated by pillars or placed on a metal cake stand should be placed on cake drums, usually 3 inches (7.5 cm) larger than the cake. For the base cake, a drum 4 inches (10 cm) larger than the cake can be used.
- Most pillars are approximately 3–4 inches (7.5–10 cm) tall so you should consider the balance of your tiered design when choosing the size of each cake. Metal stands vary in height.
- If you are stacking cakes, each tier needs to be placed on a cake board the same size as the cake ready for doweling (see pages 42–43).

These are only guidelines and a lot will depend on your design, for example if the tiers are going to be offset. The height of the top decoration often plays a big part in this decision too. Sometimes a 4-inch (10 cm) gap between tiers works well, for example for a two-tier fondant cake where a floral display needs extra space to trail. At first it can be a daunting task to make the right decision — but you will gradually build up confidence and be decisive about which formula works best for you. Remember, displays can be varied and what is pleasing to your eye is often confirmation of a correct judgment.

Pink blossom wedding cake
This pretty cake has been stacked with ribbon-covered cake drums between each layer. Doweling the cake or using a metal stand (bottom left) produces a different effect.

Countless options
When designing tiered cakes, there are lots of options available, whether you want something classic, with pillars, or quirky, such as sloping or offset tiers.

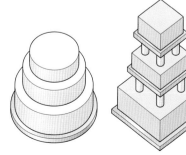
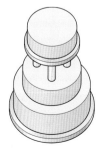
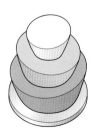

Assembling tiered cakes

The overall effect of an elaborately decorated cake can easily be spoiled by incorrectly positioned supporting pillars. Worse, an unstable cake not only creates enormous anxiety, it can lead to disaster. The process of assembling the cake is the last, worrying, task that has to be completed. Read through these instructions and use the diagrams to ensure that all goes well.

The diagrams here show how to work out where to position pillars on differently shaped cakes. The principles involved for most of the shapes are the same.

Templates can be made from paper or thin card. To obtain a good shape in each case, either draw around the cake pan and cut the shape out just inside the line, to allow for the thickness of the pan, or make a paper pattern following the diagrams for each shape, outlined at right. You will need to make one template the size of the bottom tier for a two-tiered cake and one template the size of the bottom tier and the size of the middle tier for a three-tiered cake.

For some shapes you can use either three or four pillars. Either method holds the weight of the tier above, and it is a matter of deciding which you think looks better.

Positioning pillars
This diagram applies to all shapes of cake. The points indicate how far each pillar should be positioned from the center of the cake for four sizes of cake. For example, on an 8-inch (20 cm) cake, each pillar should be 2½ inches (6.5 cm) from the center of the cake. This position will ensure maximum stability for the supported tier.

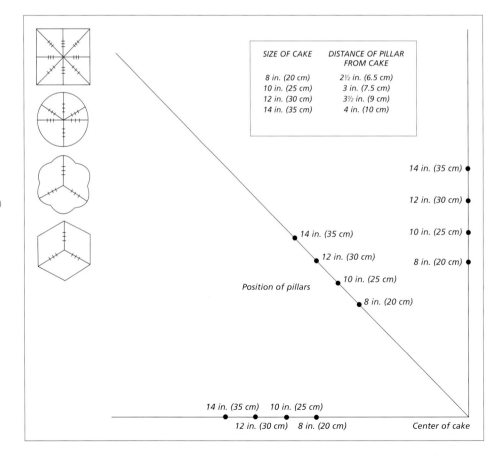

SIZE OF CAKE	DISTANCE OF PILLAR FROM CAKE
8 in. (20 cm)	2½ in. (6.5 cm)
10 in. (25 cm)	3 in. (7.5 cm)
12 in. (30 cm)	3½ in. (9 cm)
14 in. (35 cm)	4 in. (10 cm)

14 in. (35 cm)
12 in. (30 cm)
10 in. (25 cm)
8 in. (20 cm)

14 in. (35 cm)
12 in. (30 cm)
10 in. (25 cm)
8 in. (20 cm)

Position of pillars

14 in. (35 cm)   10 in. (25 cm)
12 in. (30 cm)   8 in. (20 cm)

Center of cake

Square

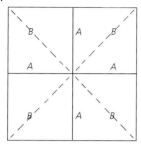

A square cake can have four pillars on the cross or on the diagonal. For the cross, fold the template into four, open it back up and mark points (A). For the diagonal, fold the square into four and then half it diagonally. Open it up and mark points (B).

Round

To obtain a round shape, fold a square into four, draw a quarter-circle shape and cut out.

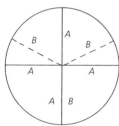

A round cake can have four pillars on the cross or three pillars on the triangle. For the cross, fold into four, open it up and mark points (A). For the triangle, fold as illustrated: fold in half and mark the first position (B) the correct distance from the center of the cake according to the chart opposite; fold into three making an angle of 60°, and mark the second position (B) on the opposite fold; open it up and mark the third point (B) on the third fold.

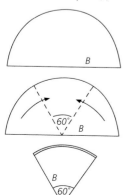

Petal-shaped

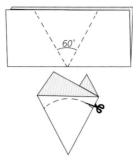

To obtain a petal shape, fold a square in half and then into three as illustrated. Draw a rounded shape as shown and cut out.

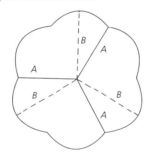

A petal-shaped cake can have three pillars, positioned on a triangle as illustrated (A or B). For (A), use the folds made for obtaining the shape and mark the points on alternate folds. For (B), fold as for the round cake and mark as illustrated below.

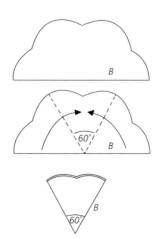

Hexagonal

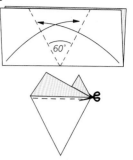

To obtain a hexagonal shape, proceed as for the petal shape but cut a straight edge rather than a rounded one.

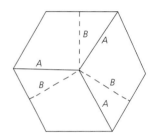

Mark the positions for the pillars (A or B) as for the petal-shaped cake, as illustrated below.

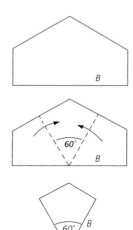

2-D designs

Motif designs, such as lettering, stenciling, piping, and fondant and gum-paste designs, can be positioned and combined in an almost infinite variety of ways to make your cake a unique creation.

Motif positions

Large, central
Make a feature of one motif. Enlarge it to a suitable size for the finished cake.

Off-center
Your cake design does not have to be symmetrical — play with ideas.

Small, repeated
Make many small identical motifs for a completely different effect.

Different sizes (same motif)
The same motif in an array of sizes gives the effect of perspective.

Repeated around the sides
Small motifs repeated around the sides of a cake provide a neat finish.

Different motifs on a theme
Try grouping motifs together, linking them by shape, theme or in a random formation.

Side plaque
A side plaque provides a focal point, to which a message could be added.

Design incorporating text
Some motifs lend themselves to displaying a message, or you can incorporate piped letters into your design.

Cupcake design

Cupcakes have become so popular that there is an enormous range of cupcake liners available. No longer are they only available in white, gold and silver — now you can buy every color under the sun, along with animal prints, stripes, stars, flowers and hearts. A range of cupcake wrappers is also now available; these fit over the top of the cupcake liners, adding a further dimension to cupcake presentation. One important thing to remember with cupcake liners is the type of cake you are planning to cook in them. While a mixture of some plain sponge and some chocolate cupcakes would be ideal for a party, using a white cupcake liner for all the cakes would clearly

show a color contrast between them when they are on the cake stand. In this case, it would be better to use darker-colored cake liners, such as chocolate brown or black, or foil cupcake liners. (If the cakes are all the same this is not an issue.) As with ribbon (see page 20), be inspired by the designs on the cupcake liners when you create your finished item. Try to plan the finished design as a whole; once you have baked your cupcakes into their liners, you can't change the color of them (unlike ribbon)!

Toppings

There is a wide range of pre-made edible toppings to go on cupcakes, ranging from sugar roses to sprinkles in all kinds of fun shapes and colors. These make decorating your cupcakes very quick and simple. Let your imagination run wild: try using favorite candies, sugar butterflies, iced flowers … The list is endless.

Ready-made decorations

The items pictured here are useful if time, energy or skill are in short supply. They can be used to add outstanding decorative effects to cakes without the commitment that many of the other sugar-craft techniques described in this book require.

Fresh flowers and herbs

Fresh flowers add instant beauty and elegance to a cake design. However, take great care to choose nontoxic blooms and foliage that has not been treated with insecticides. Also, protect your cake surface from coming into contact with fresh flowers by placing food-grade acetate on the top of the cake as a barrier. Never push flower stems directly into a cake; always use a plastic flower pick.

Silk and paper flowers

Silk or paper flowers are useful when the budget or schedule for a cake is tight. Choose smaller, prettier flowers to create a more gentle design.

Dyed skeletonized leaves

Skeletonized leaves are available from most craft stores in a large range of colors. They can be combined with fresh, silk or sugar flowers and help give floral displays a softer feel.

Beads

Beads and pearls make a great addition to sprays and bouquets. They can be wired and incorporated into your floral work. They can also be purchased ready-wired, which makes them even easier to use. Create sprays of beads using four or five different colors and perhaps a range of sizes to add interest. Always make sure the beads are secure on the wires and that they are carefully removed before cutting the cake.

Ribbons

The color of ribbon you use on your cake can have quite a dramatic effect on the overall finish. Using the right shade of ribbon can really enhance the decorations on the cake. Ribbons are a good way of incorporating strong colors, such as teal, which would otherwise be tricky to incorporate into natural-looking flowers but may be required for a special occasion, such as a wedding with teal-colored bridesmaids' dresses. Most cake drums are $5/8$ inch (15 mm) in width, so this is a really popular size of ribbon to use, whereas wider ribbons, for example 1–1¼ inches (25–30 mm), work for tying bows around the edges of cakes.

Metallic and pearlized dragées

Edible metallic dragée decorations are available in gold, silver, pink, blue and green. You can buy pearlized dragées from specialist cake decorating

stores. They are available in various sizes and can be used to create really interesting designs on the side of your cakes (see page 53).

Gold-coated chocolate hearts
Create a quick cake design with ready-made items, such as gold-coated chocolate hearts. You can also buy them in silver.

Feathered butterflies
Feathered butterflies can be used to add a fantasy feel to a floral display on a cake. There is a wide variety of styles available from craft stores.

Candy
Jelly beans, love hearts, marshmallows and any other candy can add fun and informal color if attached to a cake. For an indulgent chocolate finish, use ready-made chocolate truffles on your cake. Try wrapping them in colored foils to incorporate a color theme.

Packaging
Most cakes are given in white cardboard boxes that serve to protect the cake from being damaged or affected by the weather during delivery. Cupcake boxes are also available in a range of sizes.

CHAPTER 2

Covering the cake

Covering a cake is an extremely important basic skill. In this chapter, you will learn about the different media and methods available and how to cover your cake to form a smooth base ready for further decoration.

Tools for covering cakes

There are some essential tools that you will need in order to cover a cake. Different tools are used for specific coverings, such as fondant, chocolate paste, marzipan, buttercream and poured fondant.

Rolling pin
Used for rolling out fondant, marzipan or chocolate paste to an even thickness before applying to a cake.

Sugar shaker
Confectioners' sugar is essential for preventing fondant from sticking to your work surface as you work with it.

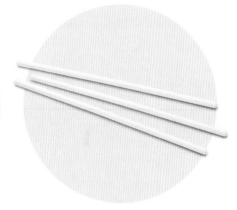

Dowels
Dowels are required to create a strong internal support system for tiered or stacked cakes that could otherwise collapse.

Palette knife
Used for spreading buttercream onto a cake ready for covering with fondant, or for applying fillings.

Pitcher or measuring cup
Pouring fondant is an excellent way of covering cupcakes. Use a pitcher to give you control when pouring.

Cake boards
These are available from cake decorating stores. They are usually gold or silver and should only be used once.

Cake smoother
Use a cake smoother to guide the fondant onto the cake instead of using your hands, which may leave fingermarks.

Sharp knife
A clean, sharp knife is extremely useful; use it to cut fondant and chocolate paste without dragging and to level out the tops of cakes.

Parchment paper
This can be used to smooth over a buttercream-covered cake and to protect the lower tiers of a cake from the cake boards above.

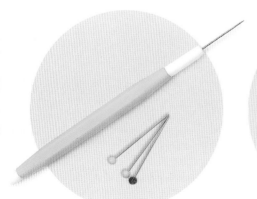

Scriber or pins
Once your cake is covered you can use a scriber (or clean, sterile pins) to gently disperse any air bubbles in the fondant.

Plastic side scraper
Run over the sides of your cake to ensure a smooth and even covering, and use to remove excess paste.

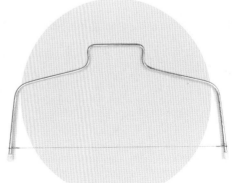

Cake leveler
A useful tool for quickly and easily cutting cakes to equal depths ready for filling with buttercream.

Covering a cake with buttercream

There are two different recipes for buttercream in this book (see page 169); both are suitable for covering cakes. You need to be careful when using buttercream so that crumbs from your cake are not incorporated into the covering. Ideally, you should cover the cake with a thin coating of buttercream and let it dry before attempting a more complete covering — this will help avoid the problem. The first coating will also seal the cake and keep it airtight and fresh. The consistency of the buttercream is important; if it is too stiff it will pull at the surface of the cake, so don't be afraid to add a little water to soften the mixture.

YOU WILL NEED

- Cake for covering
- Buttercream

- Bowl
- Palette knife
- Turntable (optional)
- Large spatula
- Jug of hot water
- Clean cloth
- Parchment paper
- Smoother

1 Soften some buttercream in a bowl with a little water, and spread the mixture thinly over the surface of the cake using a palette knife. Let it dry in the fridge for around one hour.

2 Put the cake on a turntable, if you have one. Place buttercream on the top of the cake, and spread the mixture over the cake using the spatula. Try not to let the spatula come into contact with the cake and disturb the original coating. Remove any excess buttercream.

3 Start to cover the side of the cake with buttercream using the palette knife. Hold the knife in an upright position and, with the other hand, turn the cake or pull the turntable toward you so that the coating is smooth and the covering consistent.

See also
Recipes: Buttercream **169**

4 Remove any excess buttercream. Dip a palette knife in hot water, dry it with a clean cloth, then spread it across the surface to make the buttercream smoother.

5 Alternatively, once the cake has been left to set for 30 minutes, place a sheet of parchment paper over the surface of the cake and smooth it over with your hands or a cake smoother.

Buttercream-covered cake
This cake has been completely covered and is now ready for further decoration.

TIP

If you prefer a patterned finish, carefully run a patterned smoother around the outside edge of the cake. Use a turntable if you have one, so that you can stay focused on keeping the pattern straight as the turntable moves the cake around.

Covering a cake with fondant

Covering a cake with fondant is an important skill to master, and by following a few simple steps you will be able to achieve a smooth covering for your cake. Once the cake is covered it will provide you with a base on which to apply the decorations described in this book. Applying a fondant covering will seal the cake and keep it from drying out, giving you time to decorate it over a few days. Prepare any buttercream filling at least 24 hours ahead of covering the cake to let it set and keep it from moving during the covering process.

YOU WILL NEED

- Cake for covering
- Buttercream
- Fondant
- Confectioners' sugar

- Sharp knife or cake leveler
- Palette knife
- Plastic wrap
- Rolling pin
- Sterilized pin or scribing tool
- Smoother
- Side scraper or knife

Preparing the cake
1 Using a knife or a cake leveler, cut your cake in half, ready for filling. You can experiment by increasing the number of layers and trying different combinations of fillings.

2 Place a small amount of buttercream onto your cake board to secure the cake in position. Fill your cake with a layer of filling, such as buttercream, that is approximately 1/16 inch (2 mm) thick. Don't overfill the cake, otherwise the buttercream will leak out of the sides. Place the top half of your cake on top of the buttercream.

3 Cover the whole cake with a light coating of buttercream (see pages 26–27), and cover it with a layer of plastic wrap. Let it set for 24 hours at room temperature (or place in the refrigerator for several hours). Peel off the plastic wrap, then reapply a light coating of buttercream so the cake is sticky enough to hold the fondant in place.

Covering the cake
4 Sprinkle your work surface with confectioners' sugar and roll out the fondant with a backward and forward motion, picking it up and moving it now and then to make sure that it isn't stuck to the surface. If you are unsure, use more confectioners' sugar.

5 As you roll out the fondant, you may spot bubbles of air appearing. These must be dispersed before applying the fondant to the cake. Carefully use a sterilized pin or the tip of a scribing tool to pop the air bubbles. Make sure you remove the pin from the area before you continue rolling the fondant.

7 Begin to smooth the fondant onto the cake, starting at the top. Run the smoother over the top to dispel any trapped air.

9 Run the smoother around the edge of the cake to create a smooth surface. Cut off the excess fondant with a side scraper or knife.

6 Continue to roll out the fondant until it is $\frac{1}{16}$–$\frac{1}{8}$ inch (2–3 mm) thick. Run the smoother over the fondant until it is completely smooth. If the fondant is a little sticky, sprinkle a small amount of confectioners' sugar over the surface. Lift the fondant onto the rolling pin, ready to apply it to your cake. This method is easier than lifting it with your hands, which might cause it to stretch and introduce fingerprints.

8 Carefully guide the fondant down the sides of the cake with the palms of your hands — be careful not to press too hard and mark the cake. It is important to push the fondant from top to bottom to force out any trapped air that might be under the cake covering.

Ready for decorating
A cake covered in white fondant.

Covering a cake with marzipan

Marzipan is an almond- and sugar-based paste, widely used in Europe, that can be used to cover a cake before applying a layer of fondant or for covering a fruit cake. It is not essential to use it on a sponge cake before applying fondant; however, on a fruit cake a layer of marzipan will help preserve the cake and keep any fondant applied over the top from becoming discolored. You can buy ready-made marzipan or make it yourself (see page 172).

YOU WILL NEED

- Cake for covering
- Apricot jam
- Marzipan
- Confectioners' sugar
- Clear alcohol

- Palette knife
- Rolling pin
- Smoother
- Side scraper or knife

HOW MUCH FONDANT DO I NEED?

Allow slightly more for covering a cake with marzipan, as you will want to achieve a slightly thicker finish.

Size of cake	Quantity of fondant for a round cake	Quantity of fondant for a square cake
6 in. (15 cm)	1 lb. (500 g)	1½ lb. (750 g)
7 in. (18 cm)	1½ lb. (750 g)	2 lb. (875 g)
8 in. (20 cm)	2 lb. (875 g)	2¼ lb. (1 kg)
9 in. (23 cm)	2¼ lb. (1 kg)	2¾ lb. (1.25 kg)
10 in. (25 cm)	2¾ lb. (1.25 kg)	3 lb. (1.5 kg)
11 in. (28 cm)	3 lb. (1.5 kg)	3¾ lb. (1.75 kg)
12 in. (30 cm)	3¾ lb. (1.75 kg)	4¾ lb. (2.2 kg)

1 Follow the same method as for covering a cake with fondant (see pages 28–29) with the following changes. Prepare the cake by applying a thin coating of apricot jam with a palette knife.

See also
Covering a cake with fondant **28–29**
Recipes: Marzipan **172**

TIP

Never roll out marzipan on cornstarch as this will make the marzipan ferment. Always use confectioners' sugar.

2 Roll out the marzipan on confectioners' sugar to approximately ⅛–⅙ inch (3–4 mm) thickness (deeper than fondant).

4 Using a smoother, press the marzipan down onto the cake by running the smoother over the surface and applying a steady pressure to push out any trapped air.

3 Lift the marzipan onto the fruit cake with a rolling pin.

5 Use the side of your hand to push the marzipan into the sides of your cake.

6 Cut off the excess paste with a plastic side scraper or sharp knife.

Covering a cake with chocolate paste

A popular alternative to fondant is chocolate paste. It may seem daunting to cover a cake in chocolate, but the principles are very similar to using fondant. The main difference is that chocolate paste reacts to heat. As you knead chocolate paste it will begin to heat up, especially if you are someone who suffers from "hot hands," and if kneaded for too long it will become sticky and difficult to handle. Confectioners' sugar is crucial in achieving non-sticky results!

2 Sprinkle confectioners' sugar onto your work surface and roll out the chocolate paste — keep moving the paste so that it does not stick to the surface. It needs to be rolled thicker than fondant, ⅛–⅙ inch (3–4 mm) thick, particularly when covering a chocolate cake with white chocolate paste.

YOU WILL NEED

- Cake for covering
- Chocolate paste
- Confectioners' sugar
- Buttercream
- Edible glaze or confectioners' glaze (optional)

- Sharp knife
- Sieve
- Rolling pin
- Sterilized pin or scribing tool
- Smoother
- Side scraper

1 Cut the chocolate paste into small pieces and knead each piece separately onto sifted confectioners' sugar. Once all the pieces are kneaded, incorporate them together again. This avoids any strain on your wrists from kneading chocolate paste that has become too hard.

3 Disperse any air bubbles with a sterilized pin or scribing tool. Sprinkle a light layer of confectioners' sugar onto the surface of the chocolate paste, and then run the smoother firmly over the paste to make sure it is flat and even before applying it to your cake.

See also
Covering a cake with buttercream **26–27**
Recipes: Chocolate buttercream **170**

4 Coat your cake in a thin coating of buttercream (see page 26) so the paste will have something to stick to when it is applied. See page 170 for advice on how to make chocolate or flavored buttercream.

6 Using the smoother, press the paste down onto the top of the cake and then work down the sides until it is in position.

7 Cut off the excess paste with a side scraper or knife. Be careful not to drag the paste as you cut. Use a little confectioners' sugar on the knife or scraper if this happens.

5 Lift the paste over the cake using the rolling pin to minimize contact between your hands and the paste.

Chocolate paste–covered cake
For a matte finish, leave the cake as it is. For a shiny finish, either spray the cake with edible glaze or paint on confectioners' glaze. Confectioners' glaze is an edible product used to make sugar flowers, chocolate and marzipan items shiny. It is a specialized product available from specialty stores.

Covering a cake with chocolate

YOU WILL NEED

- Chocolate paste–covered cake for coating
- Quantity of prepared chocolate ganache (see page 170)
- Confectioners' glaze
- Melted chocolate
- Royal icing (optional)
- Buttercream
- Chocolate cigarillos
- Chocolate curls (optional)
- Parchment paper
- Small cake drum
- Large palette knife
- Scribing tool
- Sharp knife
- Cake board

Once your cake is covered with chocolate paste you can add another layer by pouring chocolate ganache over it. Ganache is made up of dark chocolate and whipping cream (see page 170 for recipe). Chocolate cigarillos also make a quick and easy chocolate cake covering.

Ganache coating

1 Position the cake on a sheet of parchment paper with a small cake drum underneath it. Pour the ganache over the top of the cake and use a large palette knife to guide the chocolate down the side of the cakes.

TIP

Place your chocolate paste–coated cake onto a cake board the same size as the cake.

2 Leave the chocolate ganache to drip off the cake onto the parchment paper. If any air bubbles appear, pop them with a scribing tool.

3 Let the cake dry, preferably overnight. The cake will most likely be matte in appearance. If you would like it to be shiny, paint with confectioners' glaze. Trim the excess ganache off the bottom of the cake with a sharp knife, and carefully lift the cake onto a cake board. Fix it in place with some melted chocolate or royal icing. Try not to touch the cake, as the ganache will show fingermarks.

See also
Recipes: Chocolate ganache **170**

TIP

If you are covering your cake in white chocolate cigarillos, use white chocolate in your buttercream mix — try to match the chocolate buttercream with the cigarillos you are covering your cake with.

Chocolate cigarillos

1 These are widely available and make a quick and simple chocolate cake covering. Mix one-third melted chocolate into two-thirds buttercream to create a strong coating to hold the cigarillos in place. If the chocolate starts to set the buttercream too quickly, add a little bit of water to soften the mixture.

2 Spread the buttercream at least ¾–1 inch (2–3 cm) thick with a palette knife so the cigarillos can be embedded into it.

3 Line up the cigarillos so they rest on the cake board. Go around the cake, one cigarillo at a time, until the design is complete. Put the buttercream on in stages so it doesn't dry out too quickly.

4 Finish the cake with some chocolate curls. You can buy these ready-made or make them by crushing any cigarillos that have been damaged.

Icing cupcakes

There are several ways to ice cupcakes, and how to do it will depend on your particular design. Buttercream is one of the most common ways to ice cupcakes, along with rolled fondant, poured fondant and piped chocolate-fudge icing (see the chocolate-fudge swirl piped through a bag and decorating tip on page 55). Changing the tip will give a different effect. Cupcakes are all about presentation, so think about your design but keep it simple for really effective results.

(see the chocolate-fudge swirl piped through a bag and decorating tip on page 55)

YOU WILL NEED

- Cupcakes for icing
- Buttercream
- Decorations (optional)
- Block fondant
- Fondant
- Confectioners' sugar
- Royal icing

- Large disposable piping bag and decorating tip
- Spatula
- Plastic bowl
- Rolling pin
- Circular cutter (same size as cupcakes)
- Smoother

Buttercream

Buttercream can be either piped or spread onto a cupcake with a palette knife. With piping, the choice of tip can greatly affect the overall finish. The buttercream should be fairly stiff to keep its shape; if it is too soft, it will collapse.

Icing with buttercream
1 Place your decorating tip into the bottom of the piping bag and cut off the end of the bag so that the tip falls into place. Fill the piping bag with buttercream using a spatula — drop the icing as far down into the bag as possible.

2 Push the icing to the end of the bag, using your hand or the spatula.

3 Twist the end of the bag to keep the icing from escaping.

See also
Making a piping bag **48–49**
Basic piping: Piping swirls **55**

4 Hold the bag in an upright position and begin to squeeze. Pipe around the cupcake top in a clockwise sweep, and release the pressure when you have arrived in the center of the cupcake.

Pouring fondant
1 Heat the block fondant in a glass measuring cup in a microwave in short bursts of 20 seconds on full power, stirring occasionally, until the fondant has melted from a block into a liquid.

TIP

Be aware that if you put colored candies onto your icing, the color will "bleed" after 24 hours. Ice your cupcakes on the day you need them or add the colored candies later and attach with a little royal icing.

Butterfly cupcake
Apply decorations to the cupcake right away, while the buttercream is still soft and hasn't crusted over, so they will stay in position.

2 Slowly and carefully pour the fondant onto your cupcake until it almost reaches the top of the liner. Tap the cupcake on the work surface to remove any air bubbles, then quickly add any further decorations, as fondant sets almost instantly!

Simple and beautiful
Sponge cupcake baked in a white liner and decorated with poured white fondant and a pink sugar rose.

Rolled fondant
1 Lightly coat the top of the cupcake with some buttercream so the fondant has something to stick to.

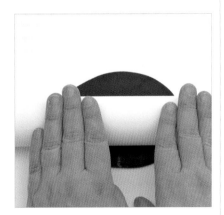

2 Roll out the fondant onto confectioners' sugar to approximately 1/16–1/8 inch (2–3 mm) thick.

3 Using a circle cutter that is the same size as the cupcake, cut out a circle of fondant.

4 Place the circle of fondant in position on the cupcake. Press the fondant down with a smoother rather than your fingers to avoid marking the surface.

5 Attach decorations to the cupcake with royal icing.

Bold design
The black fondant and pale pink sugar rose used in this design complement the highly decorative cupcake liner.

Covering a cake board with fondant

There are three different ways to cover a cake board in fondant: the "bandage" method; the "all-in-one" method, where you cover the cake and the board at the same time; and covering the board first before you put the cake onto it. The easiest method is covering the board first, but this is also a waste of fondant, as much of it won't be seen once the cake is placed on top. The quickest way is the "all-in-one" method; however, this method can be prone to trapping air and creating bubbles between the cake and the board. The "bandage" method is usually the safest option.

2 Roll out the fondant onto confectioners' sugar to approximately ⅟₁₆–⅛ inch (2–3 mm) thick, and lift it onto the cake board.

YOU WILL NEED

- Cake(s) to be covered
- Water or clear alcohol, such as vodka
- Fondant
- Confectioners' sugar
- Buttercream

- Paintbrush
- Cake board
- Rolling pin
- Smoother
- Sharp knife or plastic side scraper
- Textured rolling pin

Covering the cake board first
1 Dip a paintbrush in water or clear alcohol, and brush the cake board so it is damp.

3 Run the smoother lightly over the surface of the fondant, then cut off any excess fondant with a sharp knife or plastic side scraper, slicing away from yourself.

Covered cake board
This cake board is now ready for you to place your cake on top.

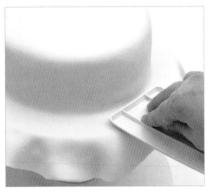

All-in-one method
1 Roll out the fondant to ¹⁄₁₆ inch (2 mm) thick, so that it is bigger than your cake and includes the extra width needed to cover the board. Coat the cake with a light covering of buttercream and run a damp paintbrush around the cake board's edge.

3 Guide the fondant onto the cake board with the smoother.

4 Cut away from yourself with the plastic side scraper to remove the excess fondant.

2 Lift the fondant onto the surface of the cake, then, with a smoother, start to push the icing into position, working from the top of the cake to the bottom.

Ready to decorate
A cakeboard and cake covered using the all-in-one method.

See also
Covering a cake with fondant **28–29**
Recipes: Fondant **172**

Bandage method
1 Roll out a strip of fondant to ¹⁄₁₆ inch
(2 mm) thick. Using a plastic side scraper
or a knife, cut a straight edge all the way
down one side of the fondant strip.

3 Guide the
straight-edged side
of the bandage
toward the side of
the cake and onto a
cake board that has
been dampened
with a little cooled
boiled water.

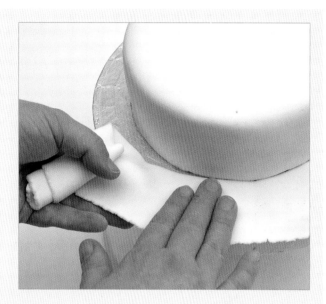

2 Roll up the fondant "bandage,"
making sure the surface of the strip is
lightly coated with confectioners' sugar
to keep the strip from sticking to itself.

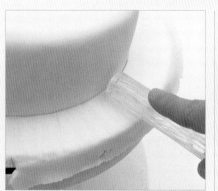

4 Using a textured rolling pin, roll over the
edges of the fondant to conceal any joins
on the fondant on the board. Be careful not
to damage the side of your cake by putting
the rolling pin too close to it.

5 Remove the excess fondant with a
plastic side scraper, slicing away from
yourself to keep the paste from dragging
away from the cake board.

Doweling a cake

If you want to stack two or more cakes, you must create an internal support system to keep them from sinking into each other and potentially collapsing. This is a straightforward procedure involving the use of doweling rods, which are available in wood or food-grade plastic. You can buy them from cake-decorating stores then measure and cut them to size using a sharp knife, or even shears. You may also need to use doweling rods if you have a heavy item to put on your cake, such as a cake topper, to keep it from sinking into the cake.

YOU WILL NEED

- Two cakes of different sizes (for example 6 inches [15 cm] and 8 inches [20 cm])
- Royal icing

- Cake boards the same sizes as the cakes
- Scriber
- Doweling rods
- Pencil or pen
- Sharp knife or shears
- Parchment paper
- Scissors
- Palette knife

1 On the surface of the larger iced cake, place a cake board the same size as the cake you want to stack on top. Mark around the edge with a scriber.

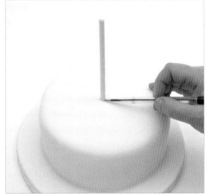

2 Place a doweling rod into the center of the cake and use a pencil or pen to mark where the dowel reaches the surface of the cake.

3 Remove the doweling rod and cut it where you have marked it. Cut five rods of identical length. If all the rods are equal the cake will be level; if they are different lengths the cake may tilt.

See also
Designing cakes: Proportions and
guidelines **15–16**

4 Push the doweling rods into the cake,
spacing them evenly.

6 Put a little royal icing
onto the top of the bottom
cake and stick on the
parchment paper. This is to
provide protection between
the cake and the cake board.

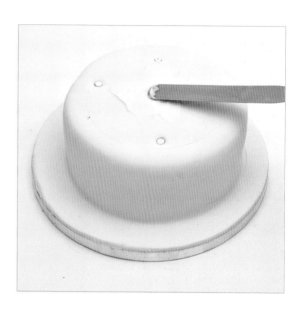

> **TIP**
>
> **Important:** The cake
> that is to be stacked
> on top of the other
> cake must have been
> iced on a cake board
> so the doweling rods
> have something to
> push against once the
> cake is in place.

5 Cut out a piece of parchment paper the
same size as the cake you will be placing
on top.

7 Put a little more royal icing onto the
parchment paper and attach the top cake
carefully, lifting it into position with a palette
knife to avoid touching the cake surface. Let
the whole thing dry for at least 24 hours.

Wedding cake
*With a strong
internal structure
you can create
beautiful tiered
cakes.*

CHAPTER 3

Piping

In this section, we look at some basic piping skills, which you can use to create simple but impressive patterns on your cakes very quickly. With a little practice, you will soon be able to create flowers, hearts, dots and much more.

Types of decorating tips

There are many types of decorating tips available for use with piping bags. Experiment with the different shapes on the market to see the amazing effects that can be achieved. Here are just some of my favorites.

Leaf tip
This specialist leaf tip could be used to create an ornate border or to add finishing touches to piped flowers.

Drop flower tip
To create impressive piped flowers quickly and easily, use this Wilton 109 drop flower icing tip.

Ruffle tip
Ruffle tips are available in a variety of shapes and sizes, such as the Wilton 100 pictured here. Use it to create plain, fluted or shell borders.

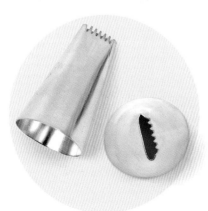

Basket-weave tip
See pages 54–55 to learn how to use a basket-weave tip to create a simple but impressive decoration.

Rope tip
This can be used to pipe small, fine borders or complex patterns; the rippled texture it produces adds interesting detail to any design.

Petal flower tip
This icing tip can be used to create the beautiful piped blossoms you will discover in this chapter.

Plastic tips
Above and below: *These large plastic decorating tips, in round and star shapes are great for piping buttercream onto cupcakes rather than finer piping.*

Medium/small writing tips
Above and below: *Round tips like these are ideal for fine piping and writing. The smallest writing tips are used mainly with royal icing.*

Star-shaped tips
Above and below: *Stars look lovely, but you will need a lot of control to pipe equal-sized stars. These special star tips are available in a variety of sizes and in open (above) or closed (below) styles.*

Making a piping bag

There are several piping bag options available. It is possible to buy disposable piping bags made of plastic. There are also washable fabric piping bags, and the traditional paper kind that you can make yourself. That process is described here.

YOU WILL NEED

- Icing, such as royal icing or buttercream (see recipes on pages 50 and 169)

- Parchment paper
- Scissors
- Decorating tips
- Palette knife
- Sterilized pin
- Damp cloth

1 Take a sheet of parchment paper, and fold one corner up to create a triangle shape.

2 Cut the parchment paper to form a square.

3 Cut along the crease to create two triangles (these will make two piping bags).

4 Take one of the triangles, pick up one of the corners and fold it up and around to the apex of the triangle.

See also
Royal icing **50**
Recipes: Buttercream **169**

TIP

Royal icing can dry up quickly and block a fine decorating tip. Keep a sterilized pin at hand to push into the tip to release any icing that has dried out. When the piping bag isn't in use, leave it to stand on a damp cloth to keep the tip from drying out.

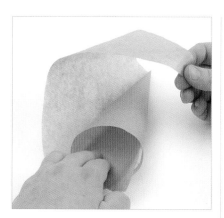

5 Holding this in place, bring the other side around and secure it by folding the parchment paper over the top.

7 Fill the piping bag with icing using a palette knife. Do not overfill the bag; keep at least a third empty.

6 Cut the end of the bag off, and drop the decorating tip into the bag. Be careful how much you cut off the end of the bag, otherwise the tip may drop out or be pushed out once you start icing.

8 Fold the top of the bag over and push the icing down into the bag, which will keep it from escaping out of the top when you begin to pipe.

Royal icing

Once you have learned how to cover your cake with fondant (see pages 28–29), the next step is to continue to decorate it, usually with royal icing — this may be piped or used to stick on fondant decorations and ribbons. Royal icing is made from confectioners' sugar, water, lemon juice and egg whites or powdered egg whites. This recipe will create a royal icing that is a medium consistency and ideal for piping work.

YOU WILL NEED

- 8 cups (2 L) confectioners' sugar
- ⅔ cup (150 ml) water
- ¼ cup (60 ml) meringue powder
- 1 tsp (5 ml) lemon juice

- Sieve
- Spoon
- Large bowl
- Small bowl
- Hand-held or stand mixer
- Spatula
- Airtight container

TIPS

- Use meringue powder when possible to avoid any risk of salmonella from using raw egg whites.
- If stored in an airtight container at room temperature, royal icing can keep for up to three weeks and be used as needed. Each time you use the icing, you will need to put the amount you want to use in a bowl and beat it with a small spatula to reinvigorate it.
- Wash and dry your mixing bowl, spatula and beaters thoroughly before commencing work. This step is important because any grease left on the equipment from a previous use will alter the final result.

1 Sift the confectioners' sugar into the large bowl to remove any lumps. Royal icing needs to be as smooth as possible; any lumps left could block the decorating tip at a later stage and make it difficult to use.

2 Pour the water into the small bowl, add the meringue powder and carefully mix with a spoon. As you mix, you will notice that the mixture turns lumpy — this is completely normal; just continue to mix for two to three minutes, then leave the mixture to settle for a further 20 minutes, to let the meringue powder dissolve.

See also
Covering a cake with fondant **28–29**

6 Turn the mixer off, scrape down the blade and immediately transfer the royal icing to the airtight container. If the icing is exposed to the air it will dry and "crust" very quickly, so keeping it covered when not in use is essential. Try to keep the icing away from the edges of your container and more as a mass to keep it from drying out in places.

3 Pour the mixture through a sieve into the confectioners' sugar. This will remove any undissolved lumps of meringue powder. Now add the lemon juice. This is added to make the royal icing more pliable.

5 After a minute on slow speed, scrape down the confectioners' sugar from the sides of the bowl, then increase the speed of the mixer to medium or high and continue the mixing process for approximately five minutes. If you watch carefully, you will be able to see the icing change from a dull white color that is soft and greasy-looking to a pure white, "peaked" royal icing.

4 Turn the mixer on at a slow speed to start with, to give the confectioners' sugar a chance to incorporate into the meringue powder mixture. Be careful to keep the speed of the mixer slow at first, otherwise the confectioners' sugar tends to escape from the bowl.

Basic piping

Piping is an important cake decorating skill and will require some practice. Buttercream and royal icing are most commonly used; here royal icing has been used to demonstrate most of the piping skills. Decorating tips are numbered by size; this varies between manufacturers. As a general rule, the smallest tip is usually a 0 or a 00. (A No. 2 tip was used for these examples.) Some tips have patterned ends. Most are made from metal, although there are plastic ones available.

YOU WILL NEED

- Buttercream, royal icing or chocolate fudge icing
- Asssorted decorating tips (plain, star-shaped and basket-weave)
- Piping bags
- Small paintbrush

TIPS

- Before starting to pipe, make sure that the icing bag has been twisted and sealed at the end to keep the icing from escaping from the top.
- Practice on a small board iced in fondant before working on a cake.
- Be careful when you wash your decorating tips — make sure that all the icing is removed (check using a paintbrush), and let them dry on a piece of paper towel.
- Some of the piping methods shown will require a slightly different consistency of icing — alter the consistency of your basic recipe by adding 1–2 teaspoons (5–10 ml) of water to find what works best.

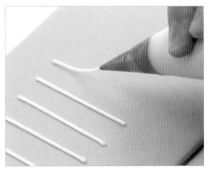

Line piping
1 Using a No. 2 decorating tip in the piping bag and some buttercream or royal icing, hold the piping bag in your right hand and support it from underneath with your left hand (or the other way around). With the tip in contact with the surface you want to ice, squeeze the bag until a little icing appears.

2 Continue to squeeze the piping bag, lifting the icing into the air so that a line is formed. Keep the pressure up, otherwise the line will break. This is quite a daunting procedure at first, but after a few attempts it will become second nature to you.

3 Place the tip back onto the surface you are decorating to complete the line of piping. If there is any excess icing or you need to adjust your piping slightly, use a small, dry paintbrush to help you. This will be the method you use to write on a cake.

See also
Types of decorating tips **46–47**
Making a piping bag **48–49**

Shell piping

1 Using a star-shaped tip on the piping bag and some buttercream or royal icing, hold the piping bag as described in "Line piping." To create a line of shell piping, place the tip where you want it, hold the bag at a 45-degree angle and start to squeeze until icing appears and begins to fan out.

2 Continue to squeeze the bag, releasing more icing, then decrease the pressure and pull the tip toward you to complete the shell. Finally, stop the pressure as the tip reaches the surface of the cake board.

3 Pull the tip away from the shell to form a tip. To continue a line of shell piping around a cake, begin the next shell so that it fans out and covers the tip of the previous shell. If you want to remove any piping you are not happy with, do so immediately with a small, dry paintbrush, before the icing sets.

VARIATION
The basic line-piping method can also be used to create a lacework or cornelli pattern. This is made up of lines of piping in a swirly pattern, close to but not touching each other. This picture shows two examples; the one on the left was piped with a No. 2 tip and the finer one on the right with a No. 1.5 tip, only available from PME.

Edging
Shell piping around the bottom edge of a cake.

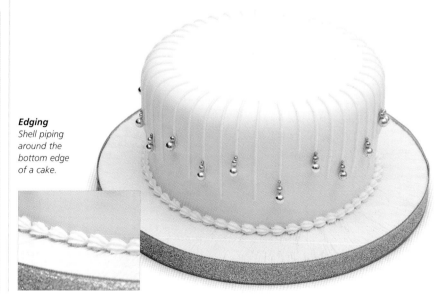

Piping bulbs, or dots

1 Using a small, plain tip, such as a No. 2, fill the piping bag with buttercream or royal icing. Hold the bag at an almost 90-degree angle slightly above where you want to pipe. Squeeze the bag, keeping the tip still. When the dot or bulb is as big as you want it to be, stop the pressure and pull the bag toward you to break the icing.

TIP

If you are using royal icing for bulb piping, add one or two drops of water before you start, to make it slightly softer, but not so soft it can't hold its shape — this will make a nice round bulb. If your icing becomes too soft add a little sifted confectioners' sugar to correct the consistency.

Piping basket-weave

1 Using a basket-weave tip, pipe three evenly spaced lines of buttercream or royal icing.

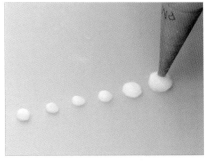

2 If you have a slight point on your dot or bulb, this can be eliminated by lightly touching it with a slightly damp paintbrush. Address this as soon as you have piped the bulb — don't leave it for more than a few minutes, as the royal icing will have set.

3 Continue to pipe additional dots or bulbs, checking the size after you have piped a few as you work. Larger dots are formed by simply adjusting the amount of icing that you are piping in one place.

2 Pipe three more lines, overlaying the first ones as shown.

3 Now pipe two horizontal lines in the gaps, as shown, to start forming the basket-weave pattern.

Piping swirls
1 Using a large plastic star tip and some buttercream or chocolate fudge icing, hold the piping bag vertically toward the outside edge of the cupcake, just inside the liner, with the tip slightly above the surface of the cake. (Using large amounts of royal icing for cupcake swirls isn't advisable, as it sets very hard and doesn't taste as nice as buttercream or fudge icing.) Start to squeeze the icing through the bag.

3 Stop the pressure and lift the icing bag directly off the cupcake to form a slight peak, if desired.

Basket
A mini piped basket made out of chocolate and containing cherries.

2 As the icing makes contact with the edge of the cupcake, move the bag in a clockwise direction until you have reached the middle of the cake.

Completed cupcake
A cupcake decorated with swirl piping with a peaked finish.

Pattern piping

When you first pipe patterns onto a cake, do it in the same color as the base. If you make a mistake you can simply remove the piped icing and make another attempt. If you are using royal icing, once the pattern is complete, let it dry for a couple of hours. You can then paint over the icing with food coloring. When deciding on a pattern, either go for something simple like piped ropes or a straight line for a clean, contemporary look, or have a look in wedding magazines for inspiration — not only at cakes, but at lace bodices, for example.

YOU WILL NEED

- Buttercream or royal icing

- Piping bag
- Patterns
- Assortment of decorating tips
- Small paintbrush

TIP

Draw your pattern on a piece of parchment paper first rather than attempting to pipe freehand right onto your cake. Pin the paper to a fondant-covered cake, then trace over the pattern with a scribing tool so that it is marked onto the cake. This can then be piped over. This cannot be done if you are piping with buttercream.

Straight-edge 2-D piping
1 This method is ideal for forming a simple box on top of a cake. Gently place a cake board on the cake to mark out the straight lines, then begin piping straight lines over the marks. Pipe two sets of lines side by side on all four sides and allow to dry for approximately 10 minutes.

2 Pipe a final line between the two lines all the way around your design. If the lines break or you need to adjust the position of the icing, use a dry paintbrush to help you — do not be tempted to use your fingers, as the icing will just stick to you.

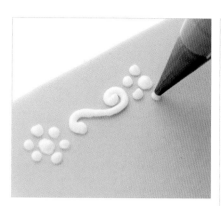

Simple daisy pattern
Pipe a central dot, then pipe five dots around it. Using the line piping technique, pipe a simple, plain scroll, moving the piping in the direction of the pattern you are trying to create.

Hearts
1 Use a No. 2 decorating tip to pipe a dot, then, before stopping, squeeze the bag and pull the tip down to form the bottom point of the heart.

2 Pipe another dot next to the one you've just done, and repeat the process for a line of hearts.

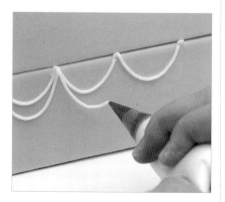

Drop loop pattern
Between measured points on your cake, pipe loops using the line piping technique. Add additional lines to the original loop to create a swag effect, or overlap the lines to create a different effect.

VARIATION
Vary the size of the heart by squeezing more of the icing out into a bigger dot or bulb. A variety of differently sized hearts can look just as interesting as a row of organized similarly sized hearts.

TIP
If you need to merge the two halves of the heart together, use a small, damp paintbrush and pull it toward you.

Piped flowers

Royal icing can be used to make quick and easy piped flowers that are ideal for decorating cakes — particularly cupcakes, when you may have a large number of cakes, for example for a wedding cupcake tower. They can also be made in advance, and once they have dried thoroughly overnight they will keep for several weeks if stored in an airtight container. You can make several kinds of flowers simply by changing the decorating tip in your piping bag.

YOU WILL NEED

- Royal icing

- Piping bag
- Wilton icing tip 109 (drop flower tip) or similar
- Waxed paper
- No. 2 plain decorating tip
- Flower nails
- Wilton icing tip 102 (petal flower tip) or similar

Flower nail
This tool is essential when piping flowers to be added to a cake.

Simple drop flowers

1 Fill a piping bag with royal icing of a medium consistency and use the drop flower tip. The royal icing must not contain any glycerin, as the flowers need to set hard. Hold the piping bag vertically and just slightly above the waxed paper, and slowly squeeze the piping bag until the icing starts to appear. Twist your wrist counterclockwise through a quarter turn to create a twist in the flower petals.

2 Stop squeezing the piping bag and lift it cleanly away from the center of the flower, leaving a small indent in the center of the flower.

3 With a piping bag of royal icing and the plain tip, pipe a dot into the center of the flower to complete it. Alternatively, you could pipe several small dots. Try piping the centers in a different color to add variation to your design.

See also
Royal icing **50–51**
Blossoms **132–133**

Piped blossoms

1 Cut out a small piece of waxed paper so it just covers the top of a flower nail, and stick it to the nail surface with a tiny amount of royal icing. Fill a piping bag with royal icing of a medium consistency, and use a petal flower tip. Squeeze the icing in the bag with your dominant hand so that it is at the end of the tip and hold the flower nail in your other hand.

2 With the wider end of the petal tip in the middle of the nail, start to squeeze the bag, moving it very slightly up and down to form a petal shape. Hold the nail still while you are piping. At the end of the petal, stop squeezing the icing and lift the tip away from the completed petal.

3 Continue to pipe four other petals in the same way to complete the flower. Using the plain tip and royal icing, pipe a center for your flower. Carefully remove the flower from the nail by lifting it off the waxed paper and placing it to one side to dry overnight. When the flower is completely dry, peel the waxed paper away. Royal icing flowers are ideal for cakes, as they are completely edible and do not contain any wire, unlike some flowers made with gum paste (see chapter 7).

Finishing touches
This cupcake was decorated with piped chocolate fudge icing and topped with royal icing flowers that were sprayed with edible silver luster spray.

CHAPTER 4

Coloring

Color is a really important part of cake decorating, and the right choices can bring your cakes to life. Here we look at the many methods for coloring different types of icing, how to use them and the different effects that can be achieved.

Basic color wheel

A basic color wheel can help give you confidence when choosing colors for your cake. Once you understand a few simple color rules, you can use them to achieve particular effects.

A basic color wheel includes the three primary colors: red, yellow and blue. These three colors, when mixed, will create all of the other colors that are used in cake decorating, but they cannot be mixed themselves. The color wheel also has secondary colors; these are colors mixed from the primary colors — orange (created from red and yellow), purple (created from red and blue) and green (created from blue and yellow). Finally there are the tertiary or "in between" colors, achieved by mixing a primary color with a secondary color — for example, red and purple. There are endless possible combinations.

Complementary colors

By looking at the color wheel you will be able to work out which colors will look lovely together on your cake and which will clash and be visually unappealing. Colors opposite each other on the wheel are called complementary colors — for example, red and green. Together, complementaries create a strong, vibrant look, rather than actually complementing each other as the name might suggest. You would combine these colors if you wanted to make something stand out on your cake, for example a green background with red glittery stars on it.

Analogous colors

Colors that are next to each other on the wheel, for example red and orange, are called analogous colors. The colors match well but don't offer much contrast.

Warm or cool?

When looking at the wheel, try to picture the finished overall effect (or mood) you would like for your cake. Colors, such as blue, green and purple, will produce a "cool" appearance, whereas reds and oranges will evoke a "warmer" feel.

Using black and white

By mixing in black and white, you will be able to alter the shade of the color you have mixed, making it lighter or darker. White coloring can also be mixed into buttercream (which can have a yellowish tinge) to make it brighter and whiter.

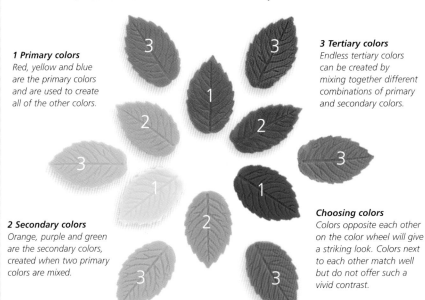

THE COLOR WHEEL
By understanding simple color rules and relationships you can achieve countless effects and moods on your cakes.

1 Primary colors
Red, yellow and blue are the primary colors and are used to create all of the other colors.

3 Tertiary colors
Endless tertiary colors can be created by mixing together different combinations of primary and secondary colors.

2 Secondary colors
Orange, purple and green are the secondary colors, created when two primary colors are mixed.

Choosing colors
Colors opposite each other on the color wheel will give a striking look. Colors next to each other match well but do not offer such a vivid contrast.

Applying spray colors

Edible food coloring is available in spray cans in a range of different colors, including metallics. This is a cheaper alternative to buying an airbrush to use with liquid food coloring, but it gives similar effects. The key to using spray colors is to be as accurate as possible and avoid mistakes, especially if you are spraying specific areas on a cake. The best way to get used to them is to try spraying single objects, such as the flowers in this demonstration. Spray colors are very versatile and can be sprayed directly onto your cake or onto chocolate, cupcakes or cookies.

See also
Stenciling: Stenciling with spray colors **105**

YOU WILL NEED

- White sugar rose
- Pearlized spray color
- Covered cake
- Clear alcohol

- Turntable
- Paper towel
- Paper
- Paintbrush

Basic color wheel • Applying spray colors

Coloring a small object
Hold the can around 7 inches (18 cm) away from the object, and begin to spray, moving in a zigzag motion across the surface.

Coloring a cake
Place the cake on a turntable. Begin to spray with one hand, using the other to rotate the turntable so the cake is sprayed evenly. Keep the can moving from side to side so the mist doesn't have the opportunity to settle in just one place.

Under the sea
This cake has been covered in white fondant and then decorated with spray colors to give the appearance of the ocean, thus complementing the chosen ribbon.

TIPS

- If you hold the can too close to what you are spraying, you will end up with a buildup of liquid that will run. However, if you are too far away you won't have much control.
- It is sometimes hard to rectify mistakes with spray colors, but a paintbrush with some clear alcohol can reduce the problem.

- Spray your items on paper towel, to absorb any excess, and in a well-ventilated area.
- To spray a specific area, mask off part of your cake with a sheet of paper so the spray will not reach the covered section. Make sure you use thick, heavy paper that is sized appropriately for your cake.

Paste colors

Paste colors are the strongest concentrated form of color available to use in sugar-craft. They have a jelly-like consistency, and, unlike liquid food coloring, a tiny amount goes a very long way. Paste colors can be used in fondant, buttercream, royal icing, chocolate paste and marzipan. They can also be diluted with clear alcohol and used to paint directly onto a cake.

One of the key things to remember when using paste colors is that the color will always dry a few shades darker than it looks when it is freshly incorporated into your icing. However, if you want to achieve very strong colors, such as red or black, it is better to buy fondant that has already been colored — mixing in large quantities of paste color is not only very messy, it can alter the consistency of the icing. For example, it can make fondant more stretchy and difficult to roll out. If your hands get covered in paste color, rinse them under the faucet with some soap. Your hands may be stained initially, but the color will soon wear off. If you are concerned about kneading in color with your hands, try wearing a pair of latex gloves.

YOU WILL NEED

- White fondant
- Assortment of paste colors
- Confectioners' sugar
- Buttercream or royal icing
- Pink and black fondants

- Toothpicks
- Knife
- Bowl
- Palette knife
- Rolling pin

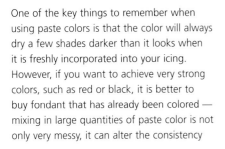

Coloring fondant

1 Take approximately 1 ounce (25 g) of white fondant. Dip a toothpick into a paste color and wipe it onto the fondant. Place the toothpick back in the pot, rather than leave it on your work surface, and dipose of it when you have finished to avoid the color transferring to other items.

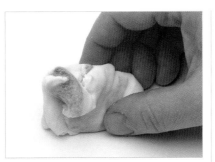

2 Knead the fondant on a work surface lightly dusted with confectioners' sugar; you will see the paste color start to incorporate. Keep kneading until you think all the color has been mixed in.

3 To check that the color is evenly mixed, take a knife and cut the piece of fondant in half. If it is all one color, it is finished; if it appears streaky as above, knead the two halves separately and then knead them back together into one piece. This is particularly important if you are mixing a dark color.

Coloring buttercream or royal icing
1 Put the buttercream or royal icing in a bowl. Use a toothpick to add the color and mix with a palette knife. Never put a toothpick back in the color after it has been in buttercream, as it will ruin the paste color.

Marbled fondant
1 Take a ball of pink fondant and a ball of black fondant (or any contrasting colors) and, on a surface dusted with confectioners' sugar, roll each one out until they are long tube shapes.

2 Place the two lengths side by side, pinch the ends together and then twist them together. Don't worry about the lengths being exactly the same width or neatly tightened — this isn't a completed decoration, just a coloring technique.

2 Press the icing against the edge of the bowl to see if the color is fully incorporated. Be careful with paste colors, as they can create lumps; look out for these as you mix the color through.

3 Fold the two twisted lengths together and begin to roll them out. As you roll you will see the marbled effect start to appear.

Using dusting colors

Dusting colors are edible food colors in powder form. There are an enormous range of colors available, or you can create your own shades by mixing colors together. The colors are available in matte or with shimmer or glitter effects.

Dusting colors can be used either in a dry form with a dry paintbrush, or, for more control and a more defined effect, mix a small amount of the powder with a clear alcohol, such as vodka; don't worry, you won't be able to taste it on your sugar creations. These colors go a long way, so be careful not to overload your brush, and always dust your designs over a piece of paper towel. Any excess powder left behind can be put back into the container.

Applications

Here, powders have been layered to pattern a gum paste butterfly. Dusting powders are indispensable for all kinds of decorations. Beginners can buy a simple starter kit and then mix their own range of colors.

YOU WILL NEED

- Selection of dusting powders
- Gum paste decorations
- Clear alcohol, such as vodka

- Various sizes of paintbrushes
- Small dish

See also
Stenciling: Stenciling with food coloring **104–105**

Basic application
1 Pour a small amount of the dust in a dish. Dip the paintbrush into the powder, tap the brush on the side of the dish to remove any excess and then gently apply the dust to your subject. If you make all of your decorations in white first, then it is simple to apply whatever color dusting powders you like.

Detailed designs
1 To paint more defined detail, add a drop of clear alcohol to the dusting powder and gently mix.

2 Paint the detail onto the butterfly slowly and carefully. If you make a mistake, dip a clean paintbrush into the clear alcohol and wipe over the error.

2 For a two-tone effect, first brush the whole butterfly with a light pink dusting powder, and then brush the center of the butterfly with a darker pink dusting powder.

TIPS
- Use a photo as reference if you want to recreate specific, realistic colors.
- Toothpicks for adding color and a small painter's palette for mixing colors and drying small items are good basics to have in your toolbox. When color mixing, always add dark color to light, never the other way around.

Fine details
To add fine details, such as the blue spots, use a small brush dipped in clear alcohol, such as vodka (which will not affect the taste).

CHAPTER 5

Sugar-craft techniques

Now that the essential skills have been established you can really let your imagination come to life and create some wonderful, unique pieces. Practice the basic techniques first, and then start to put your own creative stamp on your cakes: introduce different designs, shapes and colors and be inspired by the huge range of equipment that is available!

Types of molds

Cake decorating molds are available in silicone, plastic and polycarbonate. Whichever type of mold you choose, you will be inspired by the huge variety of shapes on the market.

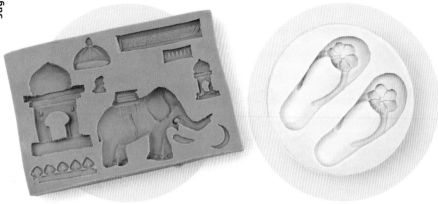

Silicone molds
***Above and below:** The most popular molds are made of silicone — these are flexible, easy to extract fondant creations from and available in all shapes and sizes.*

Flower molds
***Above and below:** Molds are available in a wide range of flower shapes but there are also many tools available specifically for creating sugar flowers, which can be found in chapter 7.*

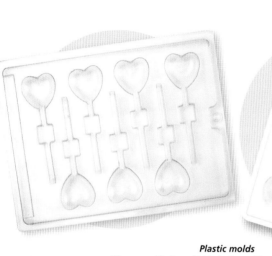

Plastic molds
Above and below: *Rigid plastic molds are now more often used for chocolate rather than fondant or gum paste due to their lack of flexibility.*

Polycarbonate molds
These are solid, hard wearing and quite expensive; they are more suited for use with chocolate than fondant.

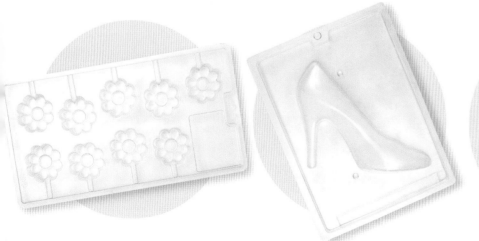

Beadmaker
This silicone beadmaker is a fantastic tool for easily making strings of fondant or chocolate-paste beads to add to your cakes.

Using silicone molds

Silicone molds are made of a soft, flexible, food-safe rubber. They are quick and simple to use, even for complete beginners, and create instant edible results to add to cake designs. Silicone molds are available in a variety of designs, from hearts and flowers to snowmen and pirates. Silicone molds work well with fondant mixed 50:50 with gum paste or chocolate paste. A light dusting of confectioners' sugar into the mold will also help with the release of the molded item.

YOU WILL NEED

- Confectioners' sugar
- Fondant and gum paste
- Chocolate paste
- Dusting colors
- Clear alcohol, such as vodka

- Selection of molds
- Small rolling pin (optional)
- Small palette knife
- Paintbrush
- Small dish

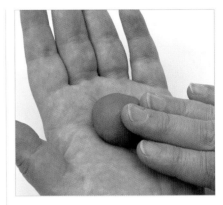

1 Roll a small ball of paste in your hand, roughly the size of the impression you want to make in the mold.

2 Sprinkle a light layer of confectioners' sugar into the mold to help the release of your molded item.

See also
Using dusting colors **66–67**
Cattleya orchid **146–149**

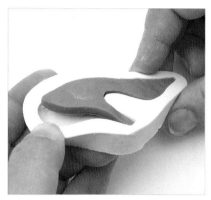

3 Using your thumb or a small rolling pin, gently press the paste into the mold.

4 Remove any excess paste with a small palette knife, so that the paste is flush with the surface of the mold. Use a sawing action from the center of the paste outward.

5 Gently flex the mold and then release the formed impression. If you are struggling to release the fondant, put the filled mold into the freezer to harden it.

6 Paint the molded design with dusting powders to achieve some detailed effects.

Leopard print heels
Fondant "dries" with a semi-hard, satiny smooth surface that holds up well to handling and takes dusting powders nicely. Paint a pattern (leopard print shown here) using clear alcohol, which will not affect the taste, and then apply some dusting powder.

Using molds with chocolate

The two main types of chocolate mold are polycarbonate and plastic. Silicone molds leave a dull finish on the chocolate so it is best to avoid them. Polycarbonate molds are more expensive and tend to be favored by professional chocolatiers, as they are hard wearing and — if cared for correctly — should last a lifetime. They also give a far superior gloss finish to your chocolates. However, plastic molds are available in a larger range of shapes and sizes and are ideal for home use. Both mold types require tempered Belgian couverture chocolate (explained on pages 156–157) for the best results.

YOU WILL NEED

- Tempered chocolate (see pages 156–157) — dark and white
- Colored cocoa butters — including yellow and orange
- Dusting colors

- Plastic molds (including a duck)
- Cotton balls
- Tablespoon
- Lollipop sticks
- Toothpick
- Small bowl
- Teaspoon
- Palette knife
- Piping bag and decorating tip
- Scissors
- Dry paintbrush
- Cotton gloves (optional)
- Polycarbonate ball molds
- Plastic wrap
- Side scraper
- Glass bowl
- Baking sheet

Chocolate lollipops

1 For good results you need a very clean plastic mold. Try not to touch the cavity of the mold with your fingers, or you will transfer grease, which will dull the finish of your chocolates. Polish the molds with a cotton ball to give a high-gloss finish to the chocolates.

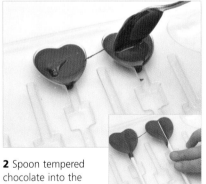

2 Spoon tempered chocolate into the mold until it is almost full. Tap the mold on the work surface to bring any air bubbles to the surface of the chocolate. Place the lollipop sticks into the chocolates and twist them so that they are fully coated in chocolate. Tap the mold once more on the work surface, and place in the refrigerator for around 20 minutes, until the chocolate is fully set.

3 Once the chocolate has set, remove the molds from the refrigerator and, using the lollipop sticks, lift the lollipops out of the mold. If the chocolate is stuck after this period of time, or the results are white or streaky in appearance, the problem is with the tempering of the chocolate (see pages 156–157).

Colored solid chocolates

1 Temper a small amount of dark chocolate and, with a toothpick, fill the eye socket of the plastic duck mold with the chocolate by dipping it into the chocolate so there is a small amount on the end of the stick.

3 Place the orange chocolate into a disposable piping bag, snip the end off so there is a small hole and pipe the beak area of the duck. If you make a mistake, use a dry paintbrush to remove any excess. Tap the mold just once to remove any air bubbles.

4 Place the yellow chocolate into a disposable piping bag, snip the end off the bag and begin to pipe the chocolate into the mold, starting at the bottom and raising the piping bag as you go so it fills completely. Tap the mold on the work surface a couple of times to allow air bubbles in the chocolate to disperse. Place in the refrigerator and leave to set for 20 minutes.

2 Temper some white chocolate (see pages 156–157). Put 2 tablespoons (30 ml) of the chocolate in a small bowl and add 1 tablespoon (15 ml) of melted yellow cocoa butter. Put 1 tablespoon (15 ml) of chocolate in another bowl and add 1 teaspoon (5 ml) of melted orange cocoa butter. Beat each color into its chocolate vigorously with a palette knife until fully incorporated.

TIP

If you cannot buy colored cocoa butter, you can color white chocolate with oil-based candy colors or dusting colors. Be careful to mix dusting colors in well, otherwise they may leave lumps of color in the chocolate.

Floating ducks
Once set, remove the chocolates from the refrigerator and unmold onto your work surface. Try not to touch the chocolates with your hands, or they will lose their gloss. If you have some cotton gloves use those; if not, handle the chocolates with a palette knife.

Hollow chocolate balls

1 Place two sheets of plastic wrap, slightly larger than the polycarbonate mold, on your work surface, and place the mold on the plastic wrap. Melt some colored cocoa butter and, with your fingertip, carefully wipe the color onto the ball molds.

TIP

Clean each individual cavity with a cotton ball to ensure the balls have a polished finish. Never use anything abrasive to clean the molds, as you will scratch the surface, and this will impact on the finished result.

4 Keeping the chocolate mold upside down, run the scraper across the bottom of the mold to remove the excess chocolate, then quickly place the mold face down on a second, clean, piece of plastic wrap.

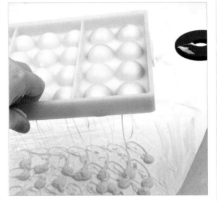

2 Pour tempered chocolate directly into the polycarbonate mold, spread the chocolate over the top and tap the mold on the work surface to bring the air bubbles to the surface.

3 Working quickly, tip the whole mold upside down so the excess chocolate pours onto the plastic wrap. Tap the side of the mold with the scraper to continue to encourage the air bubbles to disperse.

5 Wait a few minutes, then pick up the mold and scrape the soft excess chocolate off and then place it back down to set completely — about 20 minutes. The excess chocolate that was poured onto the plastic wrap will have set, and this will peel away and can be reused. After 20 minutes, the half-molded balls should come out of the molds with a light tap on your work surface. If the chocolate is not easily removed, this indicates a problem with the tempering (see pages 156–157).

6 Place some boiling water into a glass bowl, and place a clean baking sheet on top. The heat from the water below will heat the surface of the sheet.

7 Carefully take two chocolate ball halves and rub them against the baking sheet in a circular motion so that some of the chocolate begins to melt. Don't leave the balls in place for any length of time or they will melt.

9 Wipe away any excess melted chocolate with your finger to complete the ball. When you move the bowl of hot water, use oven mitts or, ideally, wait until the water has cooled completely.

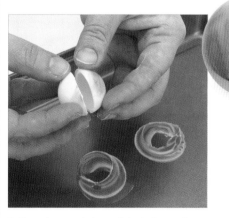

8 Place the two halves of the ball together, allowing the chocolate to set and keep the balls stuck together.

Finished chocolate balls
Chocolate balls in a range of colors can create a cascade of color down the side of a cake. Alternate plain or milk chocolate balls for a different contrast.

Using a beadmaker

A beadmaker is a piece of sugar-craft equipment made of silicone or plastic that is used to create strings of "beads" in fondant or chocolate paste. The beadmaker used here is a silicone one; they come in a variety of sizes. Start off with a ¼-inch (6 or 8 mm) beadmaker, rather than going too small. A beadmaker requires a very definite technique that, if closely followed, will enable you to produce beautiful strings of beads, which can be placed around the edge of a cake as a border or among roses to create a "vintage" look.

YOU WILL NEED

- Fondant mixed with gum tragacanth, or chocolate paste
- Confectioners' sugar
- Royal icing or sugar glue (see page 172)
- Dusting color (optional)

- Beadmaker
- Plastic side scraper
- Brush (optional)

TIP

Don't worry if you don't manage to get whole lengths of beads out each time; shorter lengths can simply be joined together when they are assembled on the cake. If you are unhappy with individual beads, cut them out and rejoin strings of beads that turned out better.

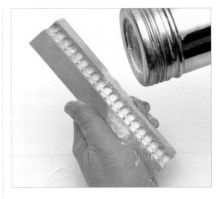

2 Place the beadmaker in one hand, open it up and sprinkle the inside with confectioners' sugar. If you washed the beadmaker prior to use, it's important to make sure it is completely dry, otherwise the fondant will stick, making it difficult to remove.

1 Roll out a long piece of fondant or chocolate paste onto confectioners' sugar. Make sure the whole piece is coated in confectioners' sugar to make it easy to release from the beadmaker. Roll the piece so that it is a bit bigger than the length of beads you are creating and approximately 1 inch (2.5 cm) longer than the beadmaker.

3 Pick up the long piece of fondant or paste in your other hand and lay it inside the beadmaker. Place the beadmaker down on your work surface and close it; the excess will appear at the top of the beadmaker.

See also
Using silicone molds **72–73**

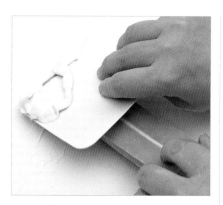

4 Cut off the excess from the top of the beadmaker with the plastic side scraper, then cut off the excess at the two ends. Cut the paste off on the top by running the scraper away from yourself. Do not use a sharp knife, or you might cut the silicone mold and damage it.

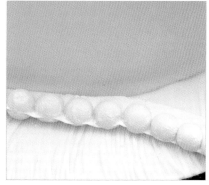

6 The beadmaker will create a line down one side of the string of beads — place this toward the back of the cake or under the beads if they are being displayed among roses. Stick the beads in position with a little royal icing or sugar glue.

VARIATION
If you want to create pearlized beads, dust the beadmaker with some dusting color before adding the fondant or chocolate paste to the mold. Pale colors work best.

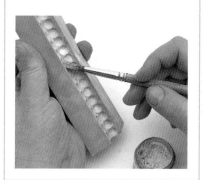

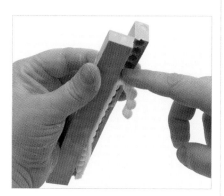

5 Turn the beadmaker upside down, so that gravity will assist you. Open the beadmaker and, with a finger, gently coax the beads out using a flicking action — do not be tempted to pull the string of beads out, as it will break or the beads will stretch.

Heart-shaped cake
Using a beadmaker gives an overall "vintage" feel to this white chocolate paste–covered cake.

Types of cutters

Cutters come in a variety of materials as well as every shape and size you can think of. There are wonderful options available no matter what your budget, level of expertise or time constraints.

Metal cutters
Metal cutters are more expensive than the plastic versions but they are sharper and extremely durable.

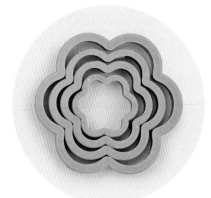

Cutter sets
Both metal and plastic cutters are available in ready-made sets. These can be different shapes surrounding a theme or one shape in a variety of sizes.

Plunger cutters
Above and below: *These come in a range of sizes and are quick and easy devices for creating cutouts, for example lots of small flowers.*

Veiners
Cutters can be combined with other tools to produce more complex sugar creations. See pages 134–135 to learn how to use veiners and cutters to create flowers.

Plastic cutters
These come in hundreds of shapes and sizes, are inexpensive and can be used to cut fondant or cookie dough thus making them very useful tools.

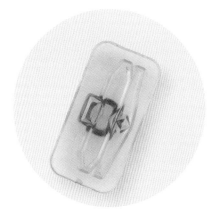

Plastic bow cutter
This multi-piece tool enables you to make intricate miniature bows, which are very impressive additions to cakes or fondant models.

Patchwork cutters
Above and below: *These versatile tools allow you to create intricate designs really easily. Use elements from a number of cutters to develop a unique design.*

Embossers
Above and below: *You can use a special embossing mat (above) or a patchwork cutter embosser (below) to create interesting patterns on fondant.*

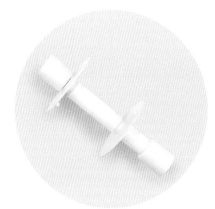

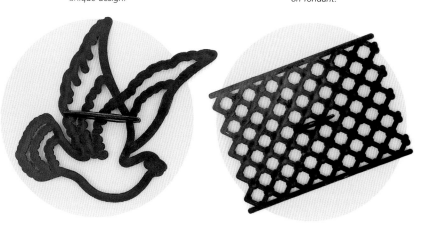

Multi-ribbon cutter
It is very difficult to cut straight strips of fondant at an equal and uniform width. Use this adjustable tool to make large bows, borders and icing panels.

*Snowflake
plunger cutter*

Using cutters

There is a huge range of cutters available to use in cake decorating: plastic, metal, tool cutters, shape cutters (e.g., cats or bows) and plunger cutters (see page 133). The most important thing to remember when using cutters is that the overall finish of your work will be infinitely more professional if the shape you have cut out has clean edges, with no excess paste. Fondant or gum paste are the main products used with cutters, although chocolate paste can also be used.

YOU WILL NEED

- White fondant mixed with gum tragacanth
- Confectioners' sugar
- Royal icing
- White gum paste
- White vegetable shortening
- Clear alcohol, such as vodka
- Edible glitter

- Rolling pin
- Metal five-pointed star cutters (in different sizes)
- Paintbrush
- Piping bag
- Snowflake plunger cutter

TIP

For this particular project, the trees have a contemporary look in white. If you prefer a more realistic tree, use green fondant, pipe on some red dots and dust with confectioners' sugar to create the impression of snow.

2 Cut out one of every size of the star cutters. In order to achieve neat edges, either run the cutter across your work surface repeatedly from left and right or, if the fondant is in your cutter when you pick it up, run your finger around the edge to remove any excess fondant. If any of the stars are stuck in the cutter, use a paintbrush to push the fondant free.

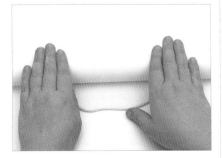

Metal cutters
1 Roll out the fondant to ⅛ inch (4–5 mm) thick. Roll out on a surface dusted with confectioners' sugar.

3 Starting with the biggest star shape, pipe some royal icing into the center and begin to pile up the smaller stars in size order (with the points alternating as shown). Each time, pipe a little royal icing into the middle of each star to place the next one on, and leave the smallest star until last.

See also
Transfer sheets on fondant **110–111**
Blossoms **132–133**

4 Pipe a small dot of royal icing onto the center of the second-to-last star and stand the last, tiny, star on its side to represent the star on top of the Christmas tree.

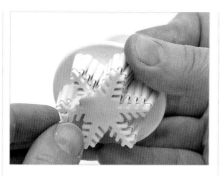

2 Push the plunger down and release the snowflake. Make as many as you need, and allow them to dry for 24 hours.

3 After 24 hours, paint the snowflakes with some clear alcohol and sprinkle edible glitter onto them. Attach them to your cake with a little royal icing.

Plunger cutters
1 Roll out the gum paste onto white vegetable shortening until it is approximately ¹⁄₃₂ inch (1 mm) in thickness. Press the snowflake cutter into the gum paste, moving it from side to side on the work surface to neaten the edges.

Christmas cake
Decorated using both metal and plunger cutters, this is a modern twist on a Christmas cake. The subtle snowflake pattern on the blue fondant was achieved using a transfer sheet (see pages 110–111).

Patchwork cutters

Patchwork cutters are extremely versatile and allow you to easily create beautiful designs. They can be used for shapes for plaques or freestanding designs or pressed into the side or top of a cake ready to be enhanced with painting or additional pieces of colored paste.

Use patchwork cutters either with gum paste or "Mexican" paste. Mexican paste is made from 1¾ cups (375 ml) confectioners' sugar, 3 teaspoons (15 ml) of gum tragacanth and 6 teaspoons (30 ml) of cold water. Knead the ingredients together and store them in a plastic bag overnight at room temperature before use. You can also emboss patchwork designs directly into fondant, which is softer and easier to mark. Try the following simple techniques, and you'll find that these cutters are a good way to increase your confidence when creating designs on your cake.

YOU WILL NEED

- White vegetable shortening
- Mexican paste or gum paste
- Sugar glue (see page 172) or royal icing (optional)
- Fondant
- Black food coloring

- Rolling pin
- Patchwork cutters — various shapes, including cat, heart, paw print
- Scribing tool
- Paintbrush
- Circular cutter
- Scissors

Using patchwork cutters
1 Lightly grease the work surface with white vegetable shortening, and roll out the gum paste or Mexican paste. Don't keep lifting the paste; let it stick to the board. Roll the paste out thinly, to ⅟₃₂ inch (1 mm) thick.

2 Run a little white vegetable shortening over the patchwork cutter edge to keep the cutter from sticking to the paste.

3 Press the cutter firmly into the paste. A clean-edged cut with no rough edges is what you are aiming for.

4 Gently lift away the cutter. The piece of paste will be left stuck to the board with the white vegetable shortening.

See also
Lettering **90–91**
Embossing and veining **106–109**

Embossing with patchwork cutters
1 Lightly grease your patchwork cutter with some white vegetable shortening by running your finger gently over the edges. Carefully press the embosser into some freshly rolled-out fondant until it is marked.

3 Decorate the embossed fondant as desired.

5 Carefully lift the cutout shape with your finger or using a scribing tool to gently coax the edges up.

2 Cut out a circle of fondant and place onto a cupcake.

6 Stick the cutout shape to your cake with a little sugar glue, water or royal icing painted onto the back.

Decorated cupcake
The embossed markings add to an original and interesting cake design.

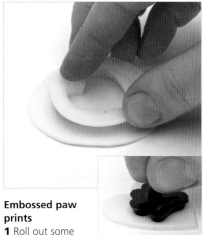

Embossed paw prints
1 Roll out some gum paste very thinly on a surface lightly smeared with vegetable shortening. Cut out a heart shape of paste. Carefully push the paw print cutter into the gum paste, so that it marks the paste but does not cut it.

Using only part of a cutter
1 Using the cat cutter from the previous page, this sequence shows how you can use part of a cutter to create a whole new design. Smear some white vegetable shortening onto your work surface and roll out some gum paste until it is very thin, allowing it to stick to the board. Using the cat cutter, cut out just a cat's head.

3 Place the cat's head motif onto a cupcake to create a fun design.

2 With black food coloring, paint in the paw print.

2 With the scissors, trim to just above the cat's collar.

Black cat
Experiment with different variations of colors in your gum paste, icing and cake liner.

Stars on wire

Stars (or indeed any other shape) on wires can add height and impact to any cake. Making them isn't difficult, but they do require some planning as they will need 24 hours to set. They are made using gum paste, which dries very hard. However, because they contain wire they are classed as an inedible item.

See also
Chocolate transfer sheets: Transfer shards **160–161**

YOU WILL NEED

- Gum paste
- Edible glitter or gold spray color (optional)

- Rolling pin
- Cutters
- Wires
- Sponge
- Paintbrush (optional)
- Plastic flower pick

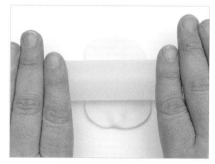

1 Roll out the gum paste to approximately ⅟₃₂ inch (1 mm) thick (not quite as thin as you would if you were making flowers), leaving a slightly raised ridge along one side that you will be able to hide your wire in.

TIP

Put a small hook in the end of the wire that you are going to insert into the gum paste to stop it from falling out.

3 If you want to add some sparkle to your cake, dip the stars in edible glitter or apply gold spray color. Group the wired stars together, and place them in a plastic flower pick pushed into the cake. Never push wires directly into cakes.

2 Cut out your shape, and push the wire into the thicker part of the shape. Let it dry for 24 hours on a piece of sponge, and make as many more shapes as you need.

Fondant-decorated cookies

You can turn plain and simple cookies into beautiful and elaborate gifts by using a variety of colored fondants and dusting colors to create some stunning effects. A range of basic sugar-craft tools can be used in a variety of ways to texture, color and add interest to your designs.

YOU WILL NEED

- Cookies to decorate
- Piping gel
- Confectioners' sugar
- Colored fondant
- Small amounts of black and white fondants
- Dusting colors and shimmer dusts

- Paintbrushes
- Rolling pin
- A selection of metal or plastic cookie cutters
- Smoother
- Modeling tools
- Small circular metal cutters

1 Apply a thin layer of piping gel onto a cookie with a paintbrush.

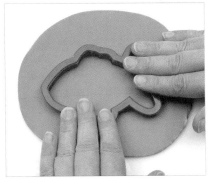

2 Roll out the fondant onto confectioners' sugar to approximately ⅟₁₆ inch (2 mm) in thickness and carefully cut out the shape.

Modeling tools
Double-tip modeling tools let you make precise markings.

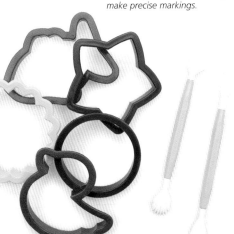

3 Shake the cookie cutter slightly on the work surface to loosen the shape and sharpen the edges.

TIP

Use the same cutters you use to cut the cookies to cut out the fondant. Cookies will expand slightly in the oven, making the fondant shape fit exactly on top with a slight border all around.

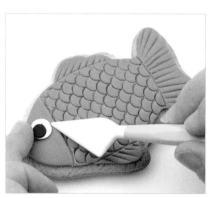

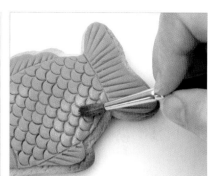

See also
Modeling tools **114–115**
Teddy cookie **120**

4 Stick the shape onto the cookie, and guide it into place with the smoother. (Using a smoother will avoid fingermarks on the fondant.) To remove any excess confectioners' sugar, lightly brush the cookie with a paintbrush.

6 Roll out small quantities of black and white fondants to approximately ⅛ inch (3 mm) in thickness, and cut out two different-sized circles for the eye of the fish. Guide the eye of the fish into position using a modeling tool (the blade tool is pictured here).

7 Brush the cookies with dusting colors to create multicolored effects. Shimmer dusts will add further interest to your finished design.

5 Using the modeling tools, create patterns on the tops of the cookies. For the fish, mark out the area for the fins using the blade, then use the scallop tool to create a scale effect, starting from one end and working across from left to right.

Sweet fish
Modeling tools can be used to create a huge range of textures and effects in fondant, from fish scales to leaf veins or brickwork.

Lettering

Creating an iced message is simple and straightforward and may be a crucial part of your cake design. It is important to use gum paste when cutting letters, rather than fondant, as they need to be rolled out very thin, and fondant would tear or stretch as you removed the letters from the cutters. Plan what you want to say and check that you have enough space on your cake. Watch your spelling, too!

YOU WILL NEED

- White vegetable shortening
- Gum paste
- Food coloring (liquid or spray)
- Royal icing (optional)

- Rolling pin
- Letter cutters
- Scribing tool or toothpick
- Paper towel
- Paintbrush (optional)
- Piping bag (optional)

Letter cutters

1 Smear your work surface with white vegetable shortening and roll out the gum paste until it is very thin. Keep lifting the paste as you roll to make sure that it is not sticking to the work surface.

2 Place the cutter down on the gum paste and cut out your letter. Move the cutter from side to side on the work surface to ensure the letter has clean, sharp edges.

3 Using the point of the scribing tool or toothpick, gently coax the letter out of the cutter from the outer edge.

See also
Designing cakes: 2-D designs **18**
Patchwork cutters **84–86**

4 Place the letters on some paper towels, and either dust or spray your letters with color before placing them onto your cake.

VARIATION
Layer letters to create a monogram of two initials. This is a popular motif for wedding or engagement cakes.

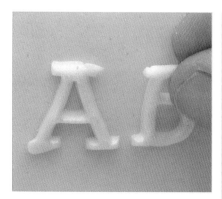

5 Letters can be placed onto your cake in two ways. If the letters have been left for several hours to dry out, pipe a little royal icing onto each letter to stick it down. If the letters are freshly cut and quite soft, paint a little water onto the back and place them into position.

Finished letters
Letters and numbers can be used to write messages and create truly personal cakes.

Sugar bows

Sugar bows can be made in lots of different ways, but here are two methods — one using gum paste and a bow cutter, and another using fondant mixed with gum tragacanth and a cutting wheel. Visually they are quite different. With the bow cutter, the size of your finished bow will be dictated by the size of the cutter, whereas the bow made with the cutting wheel is easier to adjust in size. If you don't have a cutting wheel, the bow can be cut out with a knife. Add small bows to your models, like the teddy (see pages 118–119), or use large ones to decorate the sides of a cake.

Bow cutter and a finished sugar bow.

YOU WILL NEED

- Gum paste
- White vegetable shortening
- Sugar glue (see page 172)
- Royal icing
- Fondant mixed with gum tragacanth
- Confectioners' sugar

- Rolling pin
- Bow cutter
- Scribing tool
- Paintbrush
- Piping bag
- Multi-ribbon cutter
- Sharp knife

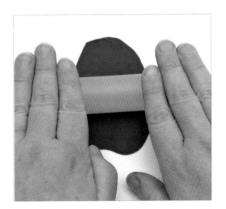

Using a bow cutter
1 Roll out the gum paste onto a surface smeared lightly with white vegetable shortening to approximately 1/32 inch (1 mm) thick.

2 Cut out the bow and remove it from the rest of the paste. It will most likely still be in the cutter, ready to be removed for assembly. Make sure the edges are clean and sharp by running your finger over the edges of the cutter to remove any excess paste.

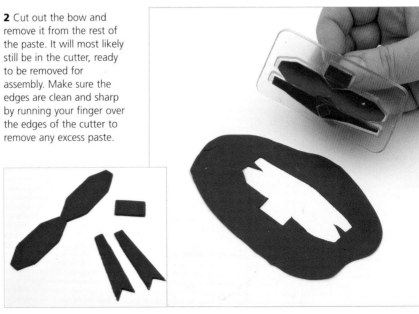

See also
Teddy **118–119**

3 Using a scribing tool, remove the largest part of the bow and place it onto your work surface, then paint the center with a little sugar glue.

5 Paint the outside edges of the wider part of the bow with sugar glue and then fold them into the center, using a paintbrush to help you guide them into position. Be careful not to squash the bow flat as you assemble it.

TIP

If the bow is squashed, use the end of a paintbrush to coax it back into shape.

4 Next, remove the tails of the bow with the scribing tool and place them carefully into the center of the bow.

6 Remove the final small square of paste from the cutter, paint the back of it with some sugar glue and position it over the join of the bow using the scribing tool to help you. Let it dry or place it directly onto your cake, securing it into position with some royal icing.

All dressed up
Sugar bows make great accessories for your fondant models.

Using a multi-ribbon cutter
1 Roll out the fondant mixed with gum tragacanth onto a lightly dusted surface of confectioners' sugar to approximately ⅛ inch (3 mm) thick.

3 Paint the back of the strip of fondant with some sugar glue, so the surface is just damp. Place the fondant strip onto the edge of the cake, using your hands to guide it into position.

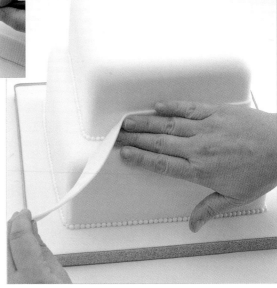

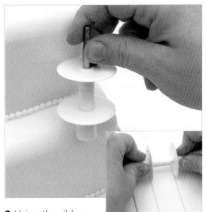

2 Using the ribbon cutter, adjust the center so that you are happy with the width of the bow you are creating. Run the multi-ribbon cutter up the fondant away from yourself. Keep it steady and try to stay as straight as possible.

4 Cut two tails at an angle for your bow with a sharp knife.

5 With some royal icing or a little sugar glue, paint the backs of the tails and place them centrally onto your cake; you can have them of equal lengths or vary them.

6 Paint another equal-width strip with icing or sugar glue and lay it horizontally across the tails. Make sure that it is straight. Fold the fondant strip into the middle to form the bow. Be careful not to crush the bow's loop. The two strips should meet exactly.

Simple style
This wedding cake is covered in white fondant and decorated with piped beads and a large bow.

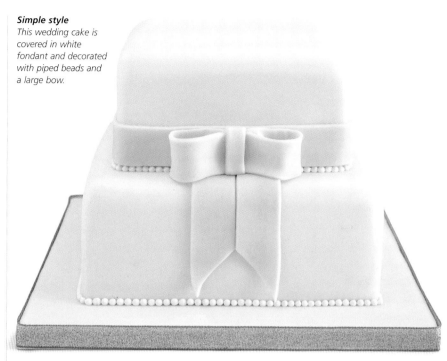

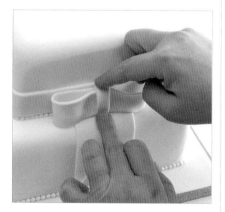

7 To complete, cut a strip of paste, paint some sugar glue onto the back and place it over the join, in the center of the bow.

VARIATION
An alternative finish would be to add a real brooch — but don't stick the pin of the brooch directly into the cake to hold it in position, as this is potentially dangerous for anyone eating the cake. Always insert the pin into a food-safe flower pick and then into the cake, or remove the pin completely and just stick the brooch on with some royal icing.

Covering a cake with icing panels

Icing panels are a modern way to decorate your cake and are also extremely useful for hiding any imperfections in the cake covering. They are made using the multi-ribbon cutter, which is capable of making very straight lines. Try varying the sizes of the panels and making them in different colors. Use a color wheel to help you decide on a color scheme (see page 62 for more on color designs).

YOU WILL NEED

- Covered cake
- Fondant in several colors
- Confectioners' sugar
- Sugar glue (optional, see page 172)

- Rolling pin
- Textured rolling pin
- Multi-ribbon cutter
- Sharp knife or plastic side scraper
- Paintbrush
- Scissors

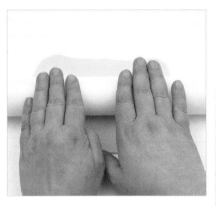

1 Roll out the fondant onto a surface lightly dusted with confectioners' sugar to approximately 1/16 inch (2 mm) in thickness.

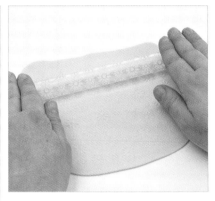

2 Roll over the fondant with a textured rolling pin.

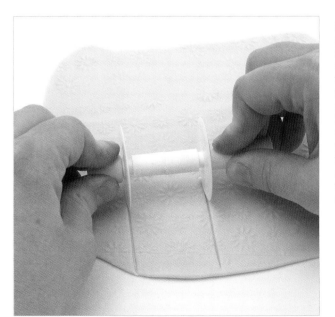

3 Using the multi-ribbon cutter, adjust the center blocks to achieve the desired width of panel. Place the multi-ribbon cutter down onto the fondant and, pressing quite hard, push the wheel away from yourself, maintaining contact with the work surface at all times.

See also
Basic color wheel **62**
Embossing and veining **106–109**

4 Cut off the end of the panel so it is sharp and straight with a knife or a plastic side scraper.

6 Pick up the panel and position it on the cake; place the panel at the very bottom edge of the cake and work upward. Use the paintbrush to guide it into position. When the panel is in the correct position, cut off any excess fondant at the top with a pair of scissors.

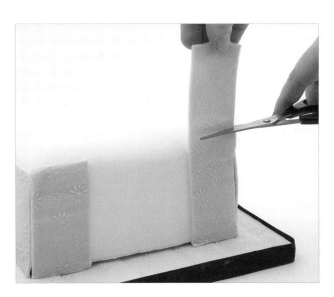

5 Turn the panel over and paint the back of it with some sugar glue or water. Make sure the panel is completely covered, but don't make it too wet.

Finished design
Adjust the center blocks on the multi-ribbon cutter and make and apply more panels in different colors, as shown.

Using a sugar-craft gun

A sugar-craft gun, also called an extruder, is a fantastic piece of equipment that can be used to create lots of different effects with fondant and chocolate paste. A sugar-craft gun is supplied with 16 differently shaped attachments, which can produce ropes (see pages 100–101), edible ribbon, writing, swirls or ribbon loops, among other things. If you find working with chocolate paste difficult because your hands are warm, this device removes the contact between your hands and the paste, making it much easier to cope with.

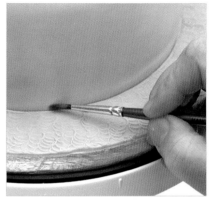

Edible sugar ribbon
1 Paint the outer edge of your cake with some sugar glue — this is to secure the fondant into position as it comes out of the sugar-craft gun.

YOU WILL NEED

- Sugar glue (see page 172)
- Fondant mixed with white vegetable shortening, or chocolate paste

- Turntable (optional)
- Paintbrush
- Sugar-craft gun
- Scissors

Fondant must always have white vegetable shortening added to it when used in the sugar-craft gun, or it will be far too hard to squeeze through. The gun works with a lever system that pushes the paste through the different attachments. It is operated with one hand, leaving your other hand free to guide the fondant into position on your cake.

Sugar-craft gun
Squeeze the handle of the gun with one hand and guide the fondant out with the other.

TIP

If you have a turntable, put the cake onto it — this will lift it closer to eye level and make it easier to see what you are doing.

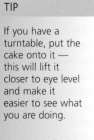

2 Insert the half-circle attachment (see detail) into the sugar-craft gun, add the fondant and screw the end of the gun on.

See also
Pattern piping **56–57**
Making ropes **100–101**

3 Push the top lever down to force the fondant to the end of the barrel, and gently squeeze the sugar-craft gun's handle so the fondant starts to appear.

Writing or creating swirls
1 Using the small circular decorating tip, load the sugar-craft gun as previously described.

3 Use the scissors to cut the fondant at the point where you wish the swirl to finish.

4 Begin to guide the fondant carefully into position with a damp paintbrush as it comes out of the sugar-craft gun. If you find this difficult, squeeze all of the fondant through the tip, cut it off with scissors and place it onto your cake with your hands.

2 Begin to squeeze the sugar-craft gun, and, with a damp paintbrush, guide the fondant onto your cake to create a swirl pattern.

VARIATION
To create 3-D curls, squeeze some fondant from the gun, using the attachment shown. Wrap it around the handle of a paintbrush and let it dry for a couple of hours. Carefully remove the paintbrush to reveal the curls.

Making ropes

Ropes give a really lovely effect on a cake, and they are much easier to achieve than it might first appear. You will need a sugar-craft gun fitted with a trefoil-shaped attachment in order to make the ropes. The ropes shown here are made with fondant mixed with white vegetable shortening — essential when using a sugar-craft gun. Alternatively, chocolate paste does not require any addition and will ease through the gun quickly and easily after a short amount of kneading.

YOU WILL NEED

- Fondant mixed with white vegetable shortening
- Confectioners' sugar
- Royal icing

- Trefoil-shaped attachment
- Sugar-craft gun
- Knife
- Piping bag

1 Place the trefoil-shaped attachment into the end of the sugar-craft gun. Load the sugar-craft gun with fondant mixed with white vegetable shortening by rolling the fondant into a long sausage. Screw on the end of the sugar-craft gun, push down the top and squeeze until the fondant starts to appear.

2 Dust your work surface with a little confectioners' sugar. Squeeze the gun until all of the fondant has been forced though the attachment, and place it down onto your work surface.

3 Cut off the fondant from the sugar-craft gun with a knife and lay it horizontally along the work surface.

See also
Using a sugar-craft gun **98–99**

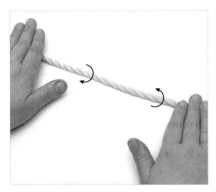

4 Place your hands at the end of each length, then roll your right hand away from yourself and your left hand toward yourself, forcing the fondant to twist into a rope shape. Continue to repeat this process until you are happy with the results. The more you roll the fondant the tighter the rope will appear.

5 Cut off the squashed ends of the rope with a knife. It is now ready to stick to your cake.

6 Pipe a line of royal icing along the edge of your cake, and then lift the rope and place it directly onto your cake. Be careful not to twist the rope, otherwise it may unwind and spoil the shape.

Complete cat cake
Ropes can be added to any part of the cake to create endless different effects.

Stenciling

Stenciling is a relatively easy technique in chocolate, buttercream, royal icing or dusting colors or sprays. To gain confidence, stencil onto pieces of fondant to make tops for cupcakes, or a sugar drape, rather than directly stenciling onto a cake, where mistakes are more difficult to rectify. If you do want to try to stencil right onto a cake, use pale colors, which will be easier to hide if you make a mistake.

YOU WILL NEED

- Fondant (for the drape, mix with gum tragacanth)
- Buttercream, or royal icing of a medium consistency
- Cupcakes
- Confectioners' sugar
- Pre-prepared fondant plaques (optional)
- Dusting colors
- Clear alcohol, such as vodka
- Spray colors

- Rolling pin
- Stencil
- Palette knife
- Round cutter
- Sharp knife
- Tape measure (optional)
- Paintbrushes
- Turntable (optional)
- Cake board
- Paper towel

Cupcake technique
1 Carefully cut out a circle from the stenciled fondant, using a cutter the same size as the top of your cupcake. Use a palette knife to lift the circle, and position the piece of fondant onto the top of the cupcake. If you wish to add more decorations, let the pattern dry for a couple of hours before positioning onto the cake.

Basic technique
1 Roll out some fondant, lay a stencil onto it and place some buttercream or royal icing (used in this example) onto a palette knife. Hold the stencil tightly in place with one hand, and glide the palette knife across the stencil in a clean sweep. Avoid pushing too hard, which will blur the pattern.

2 Carefully lift the stencil away from the fondant to reveal the stenciled pattern. Don't be tempted to touch it as it will be wet and will require a short period of time to dry.

Stenciled cupcake
Cupcake with a stenciled fondant topper.

See also
Applying spray colors **63**
Using dusting colors **66–67**

103

Stenciling

Stenciling a drape
1 Roll out some fondant mixed with gum tragacanth onto a work surface lightly dusted with confectioners' sugar to approximately ⅛ inch (3 mm) thick. Don't roll it any thinner or it will rip when you lift it to place it onto the cake. Make sure you use enough confectioners' sugar, so the fondant does not stick to the work surface.

3 Place the stencil onto the fondant and create the pattern, as described previously, with buttercream or royal icing. With a drape it is best to go for a more random pattern rather than a specific image — it will be laid onto your cake like fabric and will crease, so parts of the image could be lost, thus ruining the desired effect.

4 With some royal icing, paint the area of the cake where the drape is going, then very carefully lift your drape onto the cake and position it, trying where possible to avoid touching the surface of the drape and disturbing the stenciled pattern. Let it dry completely once it is in position.

2 Cut out your drape using a sharp knife. Either measure the side of your cake with a tape measure or, if you are confident, lift your piece of fondant up to the side of your cake to check for sizing.

Stenciled drape
Drapes can provide a splash of drama to an otherwise simply decorated cake.

> **TIP**
>
> A drape is a great way of introducing strong stenciled colors like black onto your cake without the fear of making a mistake, as the piece can easily be removed if you are not happy with it.

Stenciling onto the side of a cake

1 Place the stencil in position, keeping the edge of the stencil resting on the surface of the covered cake board so that it stays level.

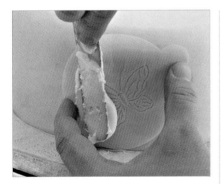

2 Holding the stencil in place, run some icing over the top of the stencil using a palette knife.

3 Carefully peel off the stencil when it is complete. If the pattern is a continuous one, wait a little while for the icing to harden.

Stenciling with food coloring

1 Place your stencil onto your cake or onto a fondant plaque. The fondant should be at least 24 hours old so it will have set and the stencil won't leave a mark.

2 Dip a dry paintbrush into the pot of dusting color, and carefully tap off the excess dust back into the pot or onto a piece of paper towel to avoid overloading your brush. This is extremely important. With a light touch, gently stipple the brush over the stencil, changing color as required with another dry paintbrush.

TIPS

- Some stencils have a very thick blank edge to them. To make it easier to stencil onto the side of a cake, you might find it necessary to trim the edge of the stencil with scissors before you begin.

- When stenciling on the side of a cake, try to use a turntable, not only so the cake is easy to turn, but so it is higher and easier to see.

3 Carefully remove the stencil with two hands, lifting the stencil straight up rather than peeling it away — this way any excess dusting color that has been left behind will be on the stencil surface rather than spread all over your cake.

For your valentine
Stenciled fondant heart ready to add to a cake.

TIP

If there is dusting color in the wrong place on your cake, you can carefully remove it with a damp paintbrush that has been dipped in clear alcohol, which you won't be able to taste. The surface of the fondant will then be slightly wet, however, once the alcohol has dried out the surface will be clear again.

Stenciling with spray colors

1 Prepare the fondant exactly as before, and place your stencil in position. Spray colors are likely to force the stencil to move when you begin to spray, so it is vitally important that you hold the stencil tightly in position.

2 Mask any areas you do not want affected by the spray, including any surface of the cake as well as other stenciled areas. Hold the spray can 3–4 inches (7.5–10 cm) from the stencil and gently spray. Don't hold the can in one position for too long, otherwise the spray will form an excess pool of color; move the can from side to side as you go.

TIP

Spray colors produce a finer, more "misty" effect compared with dusting colors, which can appear stronger.

3 Once complete, lift the stencil away to reveal the pattern.

Embossing and veining

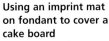

Using embossing tools or veiners is an easy way to introduce texture to your finished cake. This section shows how you can do this using a textured rolling pin or a mat with a pattern imprinted on it. They can be used to make a pattern on a bow or add detail to clothing on a sugar figure or even create a whole patterned cake. The detail can be further enhanced by painting or spraying with luster or just left as it is. The possibilities are endless.

YOU WILL NEED

- Fondant
- Confectioners' sugar
- Fondant mixed with gum tragacanth
- Royal icing

- Rolling pin
- Paintbrush
- Cake board
- Smoother
- Floral imprint mat
- Sharp knife or plastic side scraper
- Textured rolling pin
- Tape measure
- Paintbrush
- Piping bag and tip
- Tilting turntable (optional)
- Ribbon
- Glue stick

Using an imprint mat on fondant to cover a cake board

1 Roll out the fondant to approximately ¹⁄₁₆ inch (2 mm) thick on a work surface dusted with confectioners' sugar. Using a paintbrush, wet the cake board until it is just damp.

2 Lift the fondant using a rolling pin, place it onto the cake board and guide it into position with a cake smoother. Try not to touch the fondant with your fingers, otherwise you will make indentations.

TIP

You can make drapes or swags in the same way using the imprinted mat.

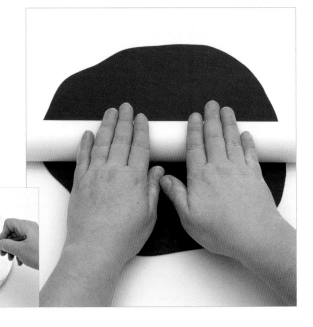

See also
Covering a cake board with fondant
39–41

3 Place the imprint mat directly onto the fondant, pattern side down, and, with a rolling pin, roll in only one direction across the fondant. Do not be tempted to roll back the way you came from, otherwise the pattern may become distorted. Take your time with this process; don't rush it.

Making a swag
1 Roll out the fondant mixed with gum tragacanth onto a surface that has been lightly dusted with confectioners' sugar to approximately $\frac{1}{32}$–$\frac{1}{16}$ inch (1–2 mm) in thickness. The fondant needs to be stretchy to keep cracks from forming during the process of creating the swag.

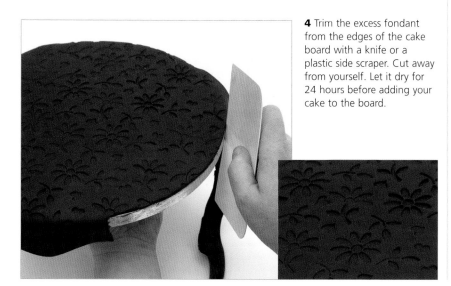

4 Trim the excess fondant from the edges of the cake board with a knife or a plastic side scraper. Cut away from yourself. Let it dry for 24 hours before adding your cake to the board.

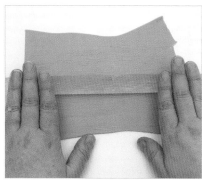

2 Roll the textured rolling pin slowly over the fondant, making sure that the fondant is marked as it goes.

Continued on next page ▶

3 Measure the gap on the side of your cake where the swag will fit, and add half as much again to the measurement so that the fondant will have enough extra length to create the swag effect.

5 Turn the piece of fondant over, and, with a damp paintbrush, fold the two outer edges over as shown. Turn the fondant back over and fold it over the top of the pattern.

7 Pinch the ends of the swag to hold it in place. Cut off any excess fondant with a knife.

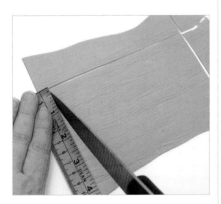

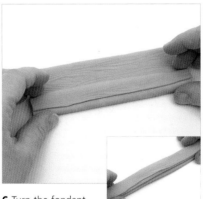

4 Cut out a piece of fondant to the correct length, using the measuring method described, by approximately 3 inches (7.5 cm) in width with a sharp knife or a plastic side scraper.

6 Turn the fondant over again, pattern side down, and then fold it over again. Finally, turn the fondant back over again, pattern side up, and fold it for a final time to create the swag.

8 Pipe some royal icing onto the side of your cake, or use water to slightly wet the cake, and then stick the swag into position. If you have a tilting turntable, tilt the cake away from you when you are sticking on the swag; this will keep the swag from sliding down the cake into the wrong position.

Attaching a ribbon
1 Run a glue stick around the edge of your cake drum.

3 Put some glue on the last piece of ribbon and stick it to the board.

TIP

Step away from your cake and examine the swags from a distance — it is easier to see if they are all hanging at the same length from a slight distance than from up close.

2 Carefully start to stick the ribbon to the cake board, checking it is level and covering the drum as you go. Cut the ribbon once the board is completely covered. Leave at least 1¼ inches (3 cm) overlapping the join of the ribbon on the board.

Swag decorations
This relatively easy technique creates impressive and beautiful embellishments.

Transfer sheets on fondant

Transfer sheets are acetate sheets with a printed pattern made of colored cocoa butter. They are normally associated with chocolate (see pages 158–161), however, using a different method, they can successfully be used on fondant too. Transfer sheets come in many different colors, and some are easier to transfer to fondant than others. Single-color transfer sheets, for example black or white, will transfer easily; sheets that have more than one color can be more of a challenge.

Transfer sheets are for a single use; once the pattern has been transferred, the transfer sheet will be blank. Practice this method of transfer onto small pieces of rolled-out fondant to start with, to get used to using the sheets and perfecting the transfer process. Have fun — there are so many types available, you will be spoiled for choice!

YOU WILL NEED

- Confectioners' sugar
- Fondant
- Transfer sheets

- Rolling pin
- Smoother
- Hairdryer or craft heat gun

1 Lightly dust the work surface with confectioners' sugar and roll out the fondant to approximately 1/16 inch (2 mm) thick. Make sure you keep lifting the fondant between each roll so that it does not stick to the work surface.

2 Place the transfer sheet down onto the fondant with the pattern pressed against the fondant.

3 Using a smoother, hold the sheet in place, so that when the hairdryer is switched on the sheet will stay still.

TIP

Move the hairdryer in a circular motion so the heat is evenly distributed over the transfer sheet.

See also
Chocolate transfer sheets **158–161**

4 Switch on the hairdryer (or a craft heat gun) and begin to heat the transfer sheet. Use the smoother to press the sheet into the fondant as you go. Hold the hairdryer approximately 3–4 inches (7.5–10 cm) away from the sheet. Keep moving the hairdryer and the smoother all over the sheet to ensure the pattern is evenly transferred. Keep heating the sheet for two to three minutes. Be careful not to overheat the acetate sheet — if this happens, it will start to crinkle.

6 When you are sure the cocoa butter pattern has transferred, peel the transfer sheet back to reveal the fondant imprinted with the pattern.

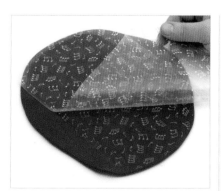

5 Switch off the hairdryer and gently peel back a corner of the transfer sheet to see if the pattern is coming off. If there is any doubt, replace the sheet and continue the process in step 4 for a further two minutes.

Festive cookies
You can find transfer sheets to suit any occasion. A snowflake pattern is perfect for the holiday season.

CHAPTER 6

Basic modeling

Creating 3-D characters on a cake is a lot of fun but can seem like a daunting challenge for a beginner. This section will take you step by step through the skills and processes needed to create some popular basic models, which you can adapt and develop as your ability and confidence grow.

Modeling tools

Raw spaghetti and a sugar-craft gun may seem unlikely bedfellows but you will find them indispensable. Team them with the great beginner collection of multifunctional modeling tools suggested below to get you started.

Sugar-craft gun
In addition to its many general cake-decorating uses, the sugar-craft gun is enormously useful in modeling. Easily create realistic-looking grass, fur or hair in no time.

Serrated cone tool
This serrated tool is perfect for modeling and shaping as well as adding texture to gum paste. Tapered cones which are not serrated are also available.

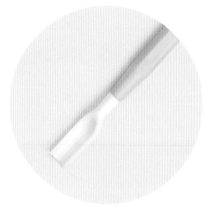

Scallop tool
This tool is great for cutting scalloped edges or circular holes, and particularly for creating neat mouths on fondant models.

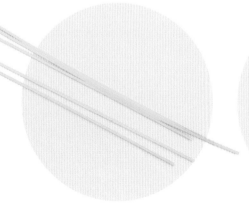

Raw spaghetti
When assembling models, it is important to have a strong internal support system to keep them together. Raw spaghetti is ideal for this.

Shell tool
Great for adding patterns or texture, this tool helps you to make the perfect shell pattern. It is also useful for marking the feet of fondant animals.

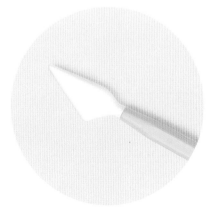

Blade tool
A blade tool is handy for cutting fondant or gum paste into whatever shape you need or trimming excess paste away.

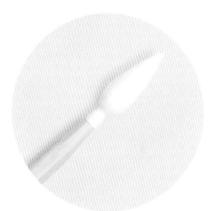

Bulbulous cone tool

A fantastic rolling tool, useful in flower work for softening the edges of leaves, and also for modeling animals and other 3-D creations.

Cutting wheel

A good way to cut straight lines and intricate shapes. Design and stitching wheels are also available, often with interchangeable heads for greater versatility.

Dresden tool

This versatile tool is used for fluting and veining. It is essential for any cake decorator, especially for detailed work.

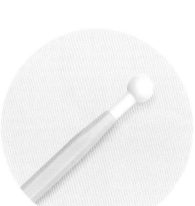

Ball tool

Great for creating indentations on sugar figurines, for example eye sockets, or an indent at the end of a sleeve to attach a hand.

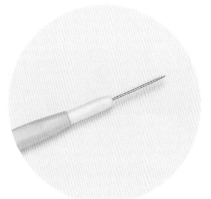

Scriber needle tool

When modeling, this tool can be used for marking very fine, intricate patterns onto your models. Always take care when using this sharp tool.

Bone tool

This is the ideal tool for smoothing curves, feathering the edges of petals and leaves and shaping gum paste items.

Bee

This is a lovely basic model to start with. It's fun and a bit different and can be displayed individually on a flower or on a cupcake — or make lots of bees and put them on a honeypot cake! This model is made from fondant that contains some gum tragacanth, which allows it to stretch during modeling, rather than cracking. A teaspoon (5 ml) of the gum powder is added to every ½ pound (250 g) of fondant, kneaded thoroughly and left overnight, so remember to plan ahead.

YOU WILL NEED

- Confectioners' sugar
- Yellow and black fondants containing gum tragacanth
- Sugar glue (see page 172)
- Rice paper
- Black food coloring

- Rolling pin
- Sharp knife or cutting wheel
- Paintbrush
- Scissors
- Modeling tools
- Toothpick
- Silver wire (optional)

TIP

Gum tragacanth is naturally occuring and great if you prefer to use natural products. You can use man-made CMC (carboxymethyl cellulose) instead for a similar effect. It works almost immediately after kneading.

1 Lightly dust the work surface with confectioners' sugar and knead the yellow fondant. Put it into the palm of your hand and roll a ball approximately the size of a raspberry; use two fingers to press against each end of the ball to change its shape and make it slightly more oval.

2 Roll out the black fondant so it is about ¹⁄₁₆ inch (2 mm) thick. Make sure you move the fondant every time you roll so that it does not stick to your work surface. Add some extra confectioners' sugar to the work surface if the fondant begins to stick.

3 Cut out thin strips of black fondant with a sharp knife or cutting wheel, carefully lift them up with your fingers and run a paintbrush dipped in sugar glue under each strip of fondant.

4 Carefully guide the strips onto the yellow body to form horizontal stripes across it. Cut off the excess fondant with scissors, making sure the join of the black fondant is at the bottom of the bee.

See also
Stars on wire **87**
Chocolate transfer sheets **158–161**

5 Use the scissors to cut out a pair of oval-shaped wings for the bee from the rice paper. Make sure your hands are dry, as rice paper will disintegrate if it comes into contact with water. Carefully push the rice paper wings into the middle of the bee, tilted at a slight angle as shown.

7 Put the toothpick into the black food coloring, so it coats just the end of it. Twist the toothpick over the edge of the pot to make sure it is clean. Push the coated toothpick into the bee where you want an eye, twist and pull it out, then repeat for the other eye. This is a much easier and more controlled way of creating eyes than trying to paint them on with a paintbrush.

6 Push a scallop modeling tool into the bee to create a smile, for a happy bee. (If you want to make your bee look grumpy, turn the modeling tool the other way around.)

8 If you want your bees to be "suspended" in the air as if in flight make a hook in a piece of wire, dip it into sugar glue and push it into the base of the bee. Use the wire to position the model wherever you like. Remember that this will make the bee inedible though; you'll need to warn anyone you give the cake to.

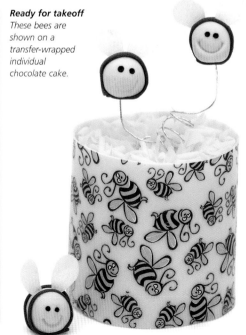

Ready for takeoff
These bees are shown on a transfer-wrapped individual chocolate cake.

Teddy

Recognized around the world, teddies are classic characters to create in sugar. Suitable for all kinds of occasions, from christenings to birthdays, they are easy to make using a few basic tools. You can make a 3-D bear or a 2-D version. If you're catering a kids' party, why not make some teddy-bear cookies (see page 120) for your guests to take home, rather than a party bag?

YOU WILL NEED

- Brown fondant mixed with gum tragacanth
- Sugar glue (see page 172)
- Small amounts of black and white fondants
- Black food coloring pen

- Raw spaghetti
- Paintbrush
- Ball tool
- Scissors
- Dresden tool
- Small circle cutters
- Stitching wheel tool

3-D teddy

1 Roll a ball of brown fondant into a cone shape, to form the body of the bear, by rolling a ball and then rolling one end only so that it forms a cone. Place a piece of raw spaghetti through the center of the cone — this is to attach the head.

2 Roll a smaller piece of brown fondant into a ball. Paint a little sugar glue onto the base of the ball, and place it over the piece of raw spaghetti. Make sure the spaghetti isn't longer than the diameter of the head before you place it in position, otherwise it will stick out the top of the teddy's head.

3 Roll out two small balls of brown fondant to form ears. Paint a little sugar glue onto the side of the bear's head, and push a ball tool into the fondant balls to form the ears. Stick them into place by pressing down.

TIP

When using the food coloring pen, be careful not to press too hard, otherwise it will dig into the fondant rather than draw on it. Sometimes it's better to leave the fondant to dry for 24 hours before drawing on details to avoid this risk.

See also
Sugar bows **92–95**
Teddy cookie **120**

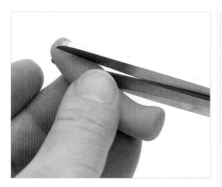

4 Roll out some small lengths of brown fondant to form arms and legs for the bear. About a third of the way down the lengths, roll with your fingers to form hands and feet. Trim the ends of the lengths off with scissors at a 45-degree angle, ready to attach to your model.

6 Using the end of a piece of raw spaghetti, gently push into the teddy's hands and feet to form paws. Be careful not to press too hard and rip the fondant.

8 Run the stitching wheel tool down the center of the bear for a more realistic look.

5 Paint a little sugar glue onto the shoulders and hips of your bear and attach the arms and legs using a Dresden tool. Mark creases where the elbows should be in the arms and where the feet are.

7 Cut out a small circle of brown fondant and attach it to the center of the face. Cut out two small white circles of fondant and two smaller circles of black fondant to make the eyes. Pinch a small piece of darker fondant to form the bear's nose. Paint the mouth of the bear with a black food coloring pen; for a female bear, add eyelashes.

The finished 3-D teddy
A 3-D fondant teddy suitable for a cake top.

Teddy cookie

It can be fun to create cookies to reflect the theme of your party, complement a cake or as gifts for your guests. This can work for any event, from children's parties to weddings, where cookies in the wedding colors could be used as an alternative to place name cards, for example. Cookies benefit from a longer shelf life than cakes, so you can confidently make them first and then focus on your cake.

YOU WILL NEED

- Cookies to decorate
- Brown fondant
- Piping gel
- Small amounts of black and white fondants
- Sugar glue (see page 172)
- Pale pink fondant
- Black food coloring pen

- Rolling pin
- Teddy cookie cutter
- Paintbrush
- Small circle cutters
- Stitching wheel tool

2-D teddy
1 Roll out some brown fondant and cut out a teddy shape with the cookie cutter. Paint a little piping gel onto a cookie and place the shape in place (see pages 88–89).

2 Roll out another piece of brown fondant and cut out a circle for the center of the face. Cut out small circles of white and black fondant for the bear's eyes. Paint a little sugar glue on the bear's face and place the circles into position.

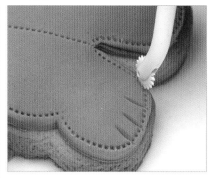

3 Use a stitching wheel to add detail to the teddy around the edge of the cookie. Cut out two small circles of pale pink fondant for the centers of the ears. Paint on the features of the bear's face with food coloring and a paintbrush or food coloring pens.

The finished cookie
A 2-D teddy cookie to complement the 3-D teddy on the cake.

Lion

This character involves a few more skills, giving you the opportunity to use more advanced equipment, such as a sugar-craft gun (see pages 98–99). As with most sugar models, the lion can be made in advance. A sugar model will keep for months or even longer in the right conditions — cool, dry and away from sunlight to keep the fondant from changing color. This can be very useful when you are planning a cake that will include‚ a number of complex models, avoiding a last-minute panic.

YOU WILL NEED

- Yellow fondant
- Sugar glue (see page 172)
- White vegetable shortening
- Dark brown fondant
- Small amounts of black and white fondants

- Modeling tool
- Paintbrush
- Raw spaghetti
- Sugar-craft gun
- Toothpick
- Cutting wheel
- Small circle cutters

Making the body
1 Roll out a ball of fondant for the lion's body, and then roll at one end to form a cone. Lay this piece on its side. Roll out another ball of fondant for the lion's head, again rolling it at one end to make a slight cone shape. Put both aside for the moment.

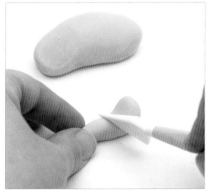

2 Roll out four lengths of fondant to form the arms and legs of the lion. For the back legs, take the lengths and bend them in the middle using the blade modeling tool, as shown.

3 Paint a little sugar glue onto the back of the lion and push the leg into position. As you do this, the fondant should spread slightly to form the hind part of the leg.

Continued on next page ▶

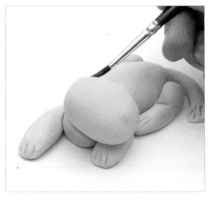

4 For the front legs, paint a little sugar glue onto the front of the lion and position one leg just under where his head will be and one next to it and slightly longer. Mark the paws of the lion on all legs with the blade modeling tool.

6 Push a piece of raw spaghetti into the lion's body, paint a little sugar glue around the base of the spaghetti and push the lion's head into position.

Details
7 Knead some white vegetable shortening into the dark brown fondant until it is soft, then load up the sugar-craft gun, using the tip with lots of small holes. Paint around the head with some sugar glue.

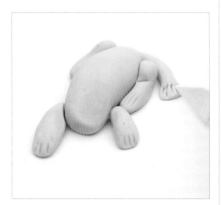

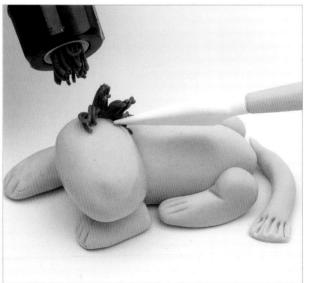

8 Squeeze the sugar-craft gun until approx ½–1 inch (1–2 cm) of the dark brown fondant appears. Using a modeling tool, such as the blade used here, remove the paste from the gun in small amounts and begin to build up the lion's mane, working in this way until it is complete.

5 Roll out another length of fondant to form the lion's tail, and mark the end with the blade modeling tool.

9 Roll out a small ball of dark brown fondant and pinch it slightly with your fingers to make it more triangular to form the nose. Paint a little sugar glue onto the lion's face and attach the nose.

11 Roll the cutting wheel over the lion's face to form the line to his nose and his mouth. At this point you can make the lion as happy or grumpy as you like!

12 Roll out white and black pieces of fondant and cut out circles to form the eyes. Stick the circles together, as shown, with a little sugar glue. Try not to position the dark centers of the eyes directly in the middle of the white balls, otherwise it will give the lion a staring expression.

10 With a toothpick, push into the lion's cheeks, to form lots of little holes, and also into the base of the nose to form nostrils.

Lion figurine
The finished character can be added to a cake as part of a jungle scene or simply on its own.

Seated figurine

Creating a sugar person is something you can really experiment with once you have mastered the basic structure. Adding, say, a beard, a different color or style of hair, glasses and various clothes — it's fun to try to replicate the recipient of your cake. Figurines are best made from fondant containing gum tragacanth, and additional supports, such as raw spaghetti or lollipop sticks will help your character to stay firmly in place, particularly if you are transporting the finished cake.

YOU WILL NEED

- Confectioners' sugar
- Black fondant mixed with gum tragacanth
- Royal icing
- Flesh-colored fondant mixed with gum tragacanth
- White fondant mixed with gum tragacanth
- Sugar glue (see page 172)
- Pale yellow fondant
- White vegetable shortening
- Black food coloring

- Knife
- Piping bag and No. 2 tip
- Raw spaghetti
- Rolling pin
- Cutting wheel
- Paintbrush
- Scissors
- Modeling tools
- Ball tool
- Sugar-craft gun and hair attachment
- Stitching wheel
- Toothpick

TIP

Always remember to tell the cake recipient if you have used an inedible product, such as a lollipop stick.

Making faces
Have fun experimenting with different features and expressions for your figures as well as accessories. Try to replicate friends, family or celebrities.

Making the body
1 Lightly dust your work surface with confectioners' sugar, take around 1 ounce (25 g) of black fondant and roll it to a 6 inch (15 cm) length. Cut off the two ends with a knife, and bend them to form legs. Stick the legs onto the cake with royal icing.

2 Roll about ½ ounce (15 g) of flesh-colored fondant into a cone for the body and then pipe a small amount of royal icing onto the legs to hold the body in place. Insert a piece of raw spaghetti through the body to the cake to strengthen the model.

See also
Using a sugar-craft gun **98–99**

3 Roll out a strip of white fondant and trim it using the cutting wheel to create a top for the character. Paint the cone with some sugar glue and wrap the white fondant around the body.

5 Roll out a long, thin strip of black fondant and attach it to the body with a little sugar glue to form a belt.

7 Roll out ¾ ounce (20 g) of white fondant into a long sausage shape, and then cut it in half to form the arms of your model. Use a modeling tool, such as the cutting wheel, to mark the creases in the elbows of your figure.

4 Trim any excess fondant with scissors from the overlap of the shirt at the back of the figurine.

6 With a piping bag, a No. 2 decorating tip and some royal icing, pipe a small square belt buckle onto the character.

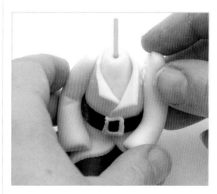

8 Attach the arms with a little royal icing or sugar glue, checking that they finish just above the knees to keep the proportions correct.

Continued on next page ▶

9 Roll ¼ ounce (10 g) of flesh-colored fondant into a ball to form the head. Push the head into position by threading it onto the raw spaghetti (make sure the spaghetti isn't longer than the depth of the head, otherwise it will stick out). Tilting the head very slightly to one side can make the model look more natural.

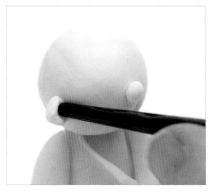

11 To make the ears, roll two more tiny balls of flesh-colored fondant. Paint a tiny amount of sugar glue onto the side of the head and, using a ball tool, gently press the center of the ear and slide it down onto the head to create an ear shape. If you are making a girl with long hair, it is sometimes not necessary to make ears.

13 Keep adding the hair until the head is completely covered. Style it with a modeling tool and trim the length with a sharp pair of scissors. If you want to create curls, you can twist it as it comes out of the sugar-craft gun.

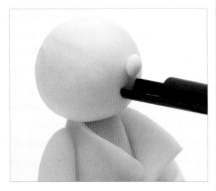

10 Create the face using the end of the scallop tool pushed into the face to make a smile. Roll a tiny ball of flesh-colored fondant and attach it with a dab of sugar glue to form a nose. Leave the eyes until last, in case you smudge them when you are attaching the hair.

12 Paint the head with sugar glue, ready to attach the hair. Use pale yellow fondant for blond hair, and mix with some white vegetable shortening to soften it for use in the sugar-craft gun. Push the fondant through the gun until it reaches your desired hair length. Using the blade tool — not your fingers — slice across the gun, catching the fondant on the tool, enabling you to lift and position it on the head.

Hands

14 Roll out two small balls of flesh-colored fondant for the hands, and then take the scissors and snip into the paste at an angle to create a thumb. Cut the center of the remaining pad straight on, and then cut either side to form four fingers. Look at your own hands to make sure the hands are in the correct position and are the right way around. If you find hands difficult to make, there are some molds now available.

15 Push a ball tool into the arms of the figurine and twist it to form a small indent, and then pipe a small amount of royal icing into the hole and position the hands just inside the sleeves. Remove any excess icing with a dry paintbrush.

Details

17 Add eyes by dipping the end of a toothpick into some black food coloring and carefully inserting it into the fondant. Remove it quickly to avoid smudging.

The finished figurine
The finished seated figurine, ready to attach to a cake top.

Shoes

16 To make simple shoes, roll two balls of black fondant and flatten one end. Paint a small amount of sugar glue onto the flattened ends and attach them to the ends of the pants.

18 Add detail to the clothes by running a stitching wheel over them to give the appearance of fabric. Be careful as you use this tool — don't press too hard or it will tear the fondant — and take your time so the pattern is accurate. It's also fun to cut out smaller strips to create pockets and other details.

VARIATION

If you want your character to stand, create the legs as in step 1, and attach the shoes as in step 11. Pipe royal icing onto the bottoms of the shoes and stand the character on the cake. Push two pieces of raw spaghetti from the waist of the legs down through the shoes and into the cake. Look at the cake from the side to check that the legs are level and not leaning before adding the rest of the body.

CHAPTER 7

Making flowers

Flowers make great cake decorations and are always appreciated and admired. You can create a huge variety of flowers from sugar, from the simple to the elaborate. Here we look at several methods so you can choose the approach that's right for you, depending on your desired result and time constraints.

Tools for making flowers

The range of flower decorations you can make is extensive — from the quick and simple to the complex and realistic — and there are specialist tools available to make each of these techniques possible.

Floral tape
Wrapping this floral tape around the wires of sugar-craft flowers will keep the wires firmly together and give a neat, realistic look.

Flower cutters
Above and below: There are hundreds of flower-shaped cutters on the market, both metal and plastic. These range from the simple and stylized to the highly detailed.

Composite cutters
Above and below: For more complex, 3-D flowers, you can use individual cutters for different petals, leaves and calyx and then assemble the parts.

Wire
Available in many gauges (the higher the number, the thinner the wire), this is extremely useful for wiring individual or sprays of flowers.

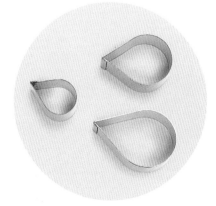

Flower picks
Plastic picks are pushed into a cake to hold wired flowers. Wire must never be pushed directly into a cake as it is not food-safe.

Veiners
Above and below: *Silicone veiners can be used to emboss a realistic pattern onto sugar leaves or petals. Available individually (above) or in all-in-one veiner and cutter sets (below).*

Foam pad
A foam pad provides a firm, flexible, nonstick surface that is ideal for molding and shaping flowers.

Scissors
It is important to have a sharp pair of scissors that can easily cut through any wire you might use in your flower display.

Paintbrushes
Making sugar flowers can require quite a lot of assembly so have small paintbrushes on hand; one to apply sugar glue (see page 172) and the other to separate petals.

Blossoms

This is a really quick and easy way to make flowers. There are several different cutters available, which will produce different types of simple blossom-type flowers. In this example, flower-shaped metal cutters and plunger blossom cutters are used. Have fun creating your own fantasy flowers and use dusting colors to bring them to life. Flowers look best displayed in odd numbers, one, three, five and so on, so keep that in mind when you are arranging them.

Plunger blossom cutters

YOU WILL NEED

- White vegetable shortening
- Gum paste mixed with gum tragacanth
- Dusting colors
- Royal icing
- Cooled boiled water
- Pearlized dust

- Rolling pin
- A variety of metal flower cutters
- Paintbrush
- Paper towel
- Piping bag
- No. 2 decorating tip
- Ball tool
- Plunger blossom cutters

TIP

When rolling out gum paste, take a small amount of white vegetable shortening and smear it onto your work surface so that it is liberally covered. This will prevent the gum paste from sticking to the surface.

Using metal cutters

1 Smear a small amount of white vegetable shortening on your work surface. Roll the gum paste to approximately $\frac{1}{16}$–$\frac{1}{8}$ inch (1–2 mm) thick, lifting and relaying it occasionally to prevent sticking. With a metal cutter, cut out shapes from the gum paste. Before releasing the gum paste, move the cutter side to side on the work surface so the gum paste is cleanly cut.

2 Once you have cut out several different shapes, carefully brush the centers of the flowers with dusting color. Don't overload your brush, or the dust will go all over the flower. Place a piece of paper towel under the flower when dusting.

3 Paint the underside of the first flower with water, and carefully lift it onto your cake. Use a paintbrush to help you guide it into place.

See also
Using dusting colors **66–67**
Using cutters **82–83**

4 Once the flowers are positioned, pipe a dot of royal icing into the center of each one with the icing bag and a No. 2 tip, and then place another cutout flower on top of it.

Using plunger blossom cutters
1 Roll out some gum paste, and brush a light coating of pearlized dust across the paste. Cut out the flowers using the plunger cutter, but do not press the plunger until you are ready to put the flower onto the cake. Make sure you move the cutter in a side-to-side motion in order to get clean edges.

3 Your flower will automatically be standing out rather than lying flat. Pipe a small amount of royal icing into the center of every blossom to complete the flowers.

5 Use the ball tool to position the top flower so it stands up rather than lying flat against the other flower. Repeat for all the flowers on the cake. Pipe another dot into the center of the top flower to complete it.

2 Pipe a small amount of royal icing directly onto the cake, and place the plunger close to the icing, so it is just touching it. Push the plunger down with your thumb; this will push the flower onto the icing and shape the flower in one go.

The finished cake
The finished cake, decorated with fantasy flowers and plunger blossoms.

Making sugar flowers with a veiner

If you look carefully at a real flower you will notice veins on the petals; these can be replicated simply and easily on a sugar flower by using a veiner. Veiners are usually made from silicone, and they can be used again and again if they are carefully washed after use. There is a range of veiners available: some come in several pieces and are suitable for pressing onto the petals while others are double-sided so that you can print veins on both sides of the flower.

YOU WILL NEED	
• Confectioners' sugar • Gum paste mixed with gum tragacanth	• Rolling pin • Sunflower Sugar Art blossom cutter (or similar) • Double-sided veiner

2 Cut out the flower shape with the cutter, moving the cutter against the work surface several times from side to side to make sure the edges are cut cleanly.

1 Dust the work surface with a light coating of confectioners' sugar to keep the gum paste from sticking. For this particular flower, roll out the gum paste to ⅛ inch (2–3 mm) so it will hold its shape once it has been pressed into the double-sided veiner.

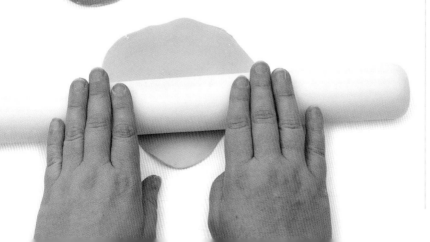

3 Dust the veiner with confectioners' sugar lightly to keep the flower from sticking to the veiner. Tap the veiner on the work surface to get rid of excess sugar.

See also
Using silicone molds **72–73**
Sugar leaves **150–151**

4 Place the flower onto the veiner with the "dipped" surface of the flower on the bottom, making sure it is carefully lined up. Push the other half of the veiner down onto the gum paste and press very hard.

6 Tip this half upside down and gently pry the flower from the mold using your fingertips. Gently stroke the flower out with your forefinger — don't be tempted to pull it or it will distort the flower.

7 Once the flower is out, let it dry upside down overnight, so it can harden and will keep its shape.

5 The veiner will now have made an indentation. Remove the top half of the veiner; the flower will be in one half of the mold.

Flower border
A large cake covered in pale pink fondant with a garland of white pearlized blossoms around the bottom edge. The flowers hang slightly below the cake for a contemporary look.

TIP

The flower can be attached to a cake with royal icing. Pipe a small dot of icing into the center of the flower to complete it.

Making a fondant ribbon rose

These 3-D roses are the quickest and easiest to make, and they are ideal for a beginner. They are best made with fondant that has some gum tragacanth in it, with a ratio of 1 teaspoon (5 ml) of gum tragacanth to every ½ pound (250 g) of fondant. This allows the fondant to stretch when the roses are folded up and keeps them from cracking. These roses work well with draping effects on a cake, as they resemble fabric. They also look chic on cupcakes, and, as they are made with a strip cutter, making many of the same size is straightforward.

Rose cluster
A cluster of different sized ribbon roses can look very effective.

YOU WILL NEED

- Fondant mixed with gum tragacanth
- Confectioners' sugar
- Sugar glue (see page 172)

- Rolling pin
- Multi-ribbon cutter
- Plastic side scraper or knife
- Paintbrush
- Scissors

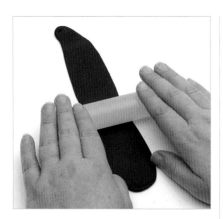

1 Roll out the fondant onto some confectioners' sugar. Try to roll the fondant as evenly as possible so that the rose will be consistent in size — it should be approximately ⅛ inch (2–3 mm) thick. Keep moving the fondant around as you roll it so it doesn't stick to the work surface.

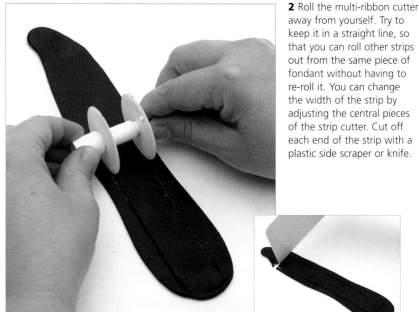

2 Roll the multi-ribbon cutter away from yourself. Try to keep it in a straight line, so that you can roll other strips out from the same piece of fondant without having to re-roll it. You can change the width of the strip by adjusting the central pieces of the strip cutter. Cut off each end of the strip with a plastic side scraper or knife.

See also
Wired sugar rose **138–142**
Chocolate fans **162–163**

3 Paint one half of the strip with sugar glue so it is just tacky, not wet, and fold the strip in half lengthwise, being careful not to crush the fold on the outside edge. Use your fingertips to completely seal the fold so it doesn't come undone.

5 Continue to roll the strip, but introduce some pleats as you go, so the rose isn't totally flat in appearance. Continue to pinch the bottom of the rose to keep it together; however, if you are having difficulty, paint a small amount of sugar glue on to help.

6 Once you are happy with the size of the rose, cut the end of the strip with scissors and paint a little sugar glue onto the end to fasten it in place. Gently bend the petals outward to cover the join and complete the rose effect.

4 Pick up the end of the folded strip and start to roll it tightly, a couple of times at first to form the center of the ribbon rose. Pinch it a little at the bottom to help the rose hold its shape.

A finished ribbon rose
The completed ribbon rose, centered on a cake for a sophisticated, contemporary effect.

Wired sugar rose

There are several ways to make sugar roses. This method uses gum paste and a five-petal cutter. It is known as the "quick" or "all-in-one" rose. It's perfect for beginners, but it requires some practice to achieve fabulous results. It is formed on wire and is therefore inedible. If you want to position the rose onto the cake on its own, do not insert the wire directly into the cake; always place a plastic flower pick in first so there is no contact between the cake and the wire.

YOU WILL NEED

- Pink gum paste
- White vegetable shortening
- Sugar glue (see page 172)
- White gum paste (optional)
- Pearlized or pink spray color (optional)
- Green gum paste

- Dark green wire
- Rolling pin
- Five-petal cutter
- Plastic wrap
- Foam pad
- Dog-bone tool
- Paintbrush
- Calyx cutter
- Scissors or cutter
- Plastic flower pick (optional)

TIP

To achieve a more realistic looking rose, start with a strong shade of pink for the center and inner petals (far right). For the next set of petals (step 12), mix the pink gum paste with an equal quantity of white gum paste to lighten it (center right). At step 16, mix the remaining lightened gum paste 50:50 with more white gum paste for the palest outer petals (right).

Rosebud
1 Before making the rose, create a cone of gum paste by rolling it in your hand. The cone should be no bigger than three-quarters the length of a petal on the cutter you are using.

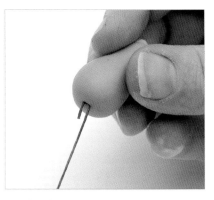

2 Make a hook on the end of the wire and push it into the bottom of the cone. Pinch the base of the cone around the wire to secure it. Let it dry overnight, so the gum paste is firmly fixed to the wire and will not fall off when you assemble the rose.

See also
Using cutters **82–83**
Chocolate roses **164–167**

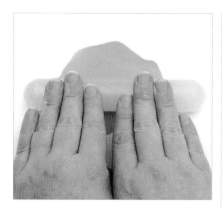

3 Smear the work surface with a light covering of white vegetable shortening, and start to roll out the gum paste very thinly, approximately 1/32 inch (1 mm) thick.

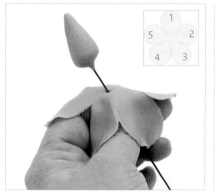

6 Push the wire through the center of the petal shape, and number the petals from one to five clockwise in your mind — this is important for assembling the rose.

7 Take petal one and cover the inside of it completely with sugar glue. Don't apply too much glue, just enough so the petal is tacky.

4 Cut out three five-petal cutter shapes. Gum paste dries out very quickly, so it is important to keep the shapes covered under a piece of plastic wrap while you are not working with them.

5 Take the first five-petal shape and place it onto the foam pad. Run the dog-bone tool carefully around the edge of every petal, half on the petal and half on the foam pad. This procedure softens the edge of each petal so the rose will look very natural when it is finished.

8 Place the petal completely around the cone, covering the tip of the cone by overlapping the petal. The top of the cone should not be seen. (Don't worry about covering the base of the cone, as the rest of the petals will cover this.) Turn the cone around so the overlap is facing away from you.

Continued on next page ▶

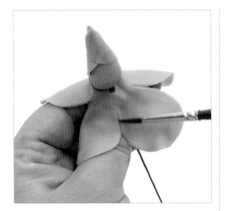

9 Paint a little sugar glue onto the bottom half of the remaining four petals.

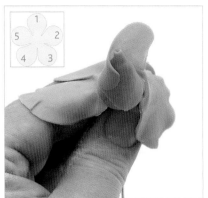

11 Glue petals three and five in the same way, interweaving them with each other, not the layer below. Try to keep each layer as tight as possible around the cone. Slightly bend back the exposed petals. At this stage you have made a rosebud.

13 Take petal three and overlap half of petal one with it. Pinch slightly and bend back each petal. Take your time to position each of the petals correctly — have the sugar glue close by in case you need to add a touch more.

10 Take petal four and glue one side to the cone, and then take petal two and glue it to the cone, interweaving it with petal four. One side of each petal should be tucked into the other.

Full rose
12 Take a second five-petal shape, place it onto the foam pad and repeat step 5 for this petal. Then turn the petal over and insert the wire through the center as before. Number the petals in your mind again, and glue the bottom third of all the petals this time. Take petal one and place it around the first layer of one of the exposed petals from layer one in the middle of the petal.

14 Take petal two over the overlap of petals three and one. Pinch slightly and bend back as before. The reason for bending the petals back is to make them look more realistic.

15 Petals four and five should overlap each other and be evenly placed around the rest of the rose. Pinch and bend back the petals as before. Add a little extra sugar glue in any places that are struggling to stay in place.

16 Thread the last remaining five-petal cutout onto the wire and paint a little sugar glue down the edges of each petal. Begin by attaching the first petal on the left-hand side.

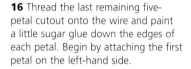

17 In order, take each petal and carefully position it so it interlocks onto the cone, until all five petals are evenly positioned around the whole rose.

18 Carefully arrange the five petals around the outside edge of the rose, and bend the petals back to make them look more realistic.

TIPS

- If you are planning to enhance the rose with further color, such as a spray color, this is the best time to do it — once it has dried and before you add the calyx. White roses sprayed with a pearlized spray look very effective, and a light spray on a pink rose will look very natural, as roses are not a uniform color.
- Once gum paste dries, it is very hard but also brittle, so avoid knocking the flowers as you are likely to damage them. The roses will keep indefinitely in a box, away from sunlight and warm temperatures. Don't keep flower sprays in an airtight box, though, as this can make the flowers "sweat," become damp and turn moldy.

Calyx
19 Roll out the green gum paste, as before on some white vegetable shortening, and cut out the calyx.

Continued on next page ▶

20 For additional detail, snip into each sepal of the calyx with a pair of sharp scissors or a cutter to create a more realistic rose. The sepals are more likely to snap if they are cut, however, so if you are unsure skip this stage.

22 Finally, take a pea-sized ball of green gum paste and thread the wire through it. Paint a tiny amount of sugar glue onto it and push it onto the underside of the rose to complete the flower.

The complete rose
The finished rose, with enough wire to attach it to the cake or to other flowers in a spray.

21 Thread the wire through the center of the calyx, paint some sugar glue onto its underside and stick it to the bottom of the rose.

A complete cake
A tiered cake complete with white wired sugar roses.

Gerbera

Gerberas are dramatic flowers, available in a huge range of colors and popular on all kinds of celebration cakes. As they are large flowers, fewer are required for a cake compared with other blooms; a single flower can form a natural focal point. A gerbera is an easy flower for a beginner, but remember to allow at least 24 hours for the flower to dry so it will hold its shape. This flower is made from gum paste and doesn't contain any wires, so it remains edible, although gum paste does set hard and, therefore, tends not to be eaten.

YOU WILL NEED

- Confectioners' sugar
- Red gum paste
- Sugar glue (see page 172)
- Black gum paste

- Aluminum foil
- Gerbera cutter
- Rolling pin
- Paintbrush
- Daisy cutter
- Cutting wheel
- Ball tool
- Sieve

1 Cut a piece of foil slightly larger than the gerbera cutter, and fold it to form a slightly dipped cup, which you will need to use to dry your gerbera in.

2 Lightly dust the work surface with some confectioners' sugar and roll out the red gum paste to around 1/32–1/16 inch (1–2 mm) thick. Lift the paste intermittently as you roll it out to make sure it does not stick to the work surface.

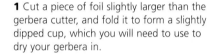

3 Sprinkle the underside of the cutter with a little confectioners' sugar.

Continued on next page ▶

4 Cut out a gerbera, moving the cutter from side to side on the work surface to ensure the gum paste cuts cleanly. Keep the cutter flat on the work surface, and press the plunger down so the petals are indented with the markings of the gerbera.

6 Paint a little sugar glue in the center of the first flower, and place the second flower on top, slightly off-center so the petals alternate and are not directly on top of each other.

5 Pick up the cutter, still containing the flower. Press the plunger on the top of the cutter down and release the gum paste into the foil cup you made earlier. Repeat steps 4 and 5 to create a second gerbera.

7 Cut out two pieces of gum paste with the daisy cutter. Using the cutting wheel, cut each of the petals in half by running the wheel from the center out to the edge.

8 Paint a small amount of sugar glue in the center of one of the smaller flowers and stick the two together, alternated, as with the large flower in step 6.

See also
Blossoms: Using plunger blossom
cutters **133**

9 Paint more sugar glue in the center of the larger flower and place the two smaller flowers into the center. Use a ball tool to position the small flowers and push down gently so the small petals curl in slightly.

11 Paint the middle of the small flower with sugar glue and place the black center into the flower. Run a paintbrush around the edge of the center. Then, using a dry paintbrush, encourage the smaller petals to stick to the center to complete the gerbera.

TIPS

- Remove any excess confectioners' sugar from your flower with a dry paintbrush.
- If any of the petals are overlapping, use a dry paintbrush, rather than your fingers, to flatten and separate them.

10 Roll a small ball of black gum paste, about the size of a pea, for the center of the flower. Press the ball lightly into the sieve to create markings.

Chic accessory
As a single flower, a gerbera can add a modern twist to a handbag cake.

Cattleya orchid

At first glance, orchids appear complex and difficult to make, but by planning your work in advance to allow some drying time, this flower is actually quite easy to make. As the orchid is so beautiful in its own right it is often displayed as a single item on a cake. This particular orchid is well known for making an appearance in bridal corsages, so they are ideal for a wedding cake. Try to work from a picture or a real specimen, as this helps with achieving accurate coloration and assembly.

YOU WILL NEED

- Confectioners' sugar
- Pale pink gum paste
- Sugar glue (see page 172)
- Pink luster

- All-in-one set of molds, cutters and veiners for cattleya orchid
- White wire
- Toothpick
- Rolling pin
- Ball tool
- Foam pad
- Paintbrush
- Mid-green floral tape
- Scissors

Making the column
1 Lightly dust the column mold with confectioners' sugar and fill it with a small cone-shaped piece of rolled pale pink gum paste. Press quite hard so the paste fills the mold and takes on the indentations, and remove any excess by smearing it away with your finger.

2 Make a small hook on the end of piece of white wire, dip it into some sugar glue and insert it about a third of the way into the narrower end of the column. To remove the column, press firmly into the mold with a slightly damp finger, and it should come out easily. If the column is stuck, try tipping it upside down or teasing it out with a toothpick. Leave to dry for 24 hours.

Making the pointed petals
3 Dust your work surface with confectioners' sugar and roll out the pale pink gum paste. Lift and reposition the gum paste as you go to make sure it doesn't stick to the work surface. Roll it until it is around 1/32 inch (1 mm) thick. Press the pointed petal cutter down firmly onto the paste, and then move the cutter from side to side for a clean cut.

See also
Using dusting colors **66–67**
Using silicone molds **72–73**

4 Lift the cutter carefully from the board and turn it over — the gum paste should be lying in the cutter. If it has come loose, pick it up and place it back in. Begin the process of veining by tapping the paste firmly into the mold so that it is embossed with the pattern. Make sure your fingers are dry, otherwise the gum paste will end up sticking to your fingers.

6 Remove the petal by dampening your finger slightly and pressing onto the petal, so that it is tacky and sticks to your finger for removal. Do not be tempted to remove the petal by pulling the wire!

7 Gently run the ball tool around the petal on a foam pad to soften the edges. Let the petal dry on a curved object, as shown in step 8. Make two more pointed petals in the same way, and dry these with the veined side up. Let them dry for 24 hours.

5 While the petal is still in the cutter, cut a small piece of gum paste, dip a piece of wire into some sugar glue and attach it to the patch. Turn the patch over and press it firmly down onto the bottom central part of the petal in the cutter.

Making the side petals
8 Cut out two side petals from pink gum paste, and vein and wire them as before. Place them on a foam pad, and gently run the ball tool around the edges to frill them. Rest the petals against a rolling pin, veined side up, and let dry for 24 hours.

Continued on next page ▶

Making the trumpet petal
9 Cut out one trumpet petal per orchid from pink gum paste, but do not wire it. Place the petal on the foam pad and, with a ball tool, gently frill the edges. If the paste cracks it may have dried out, and you should consider re-rolling. Place the petal onto the orchid stand as shown in step 11, using the ball tool to ease the petal into place.

11 Leave to dry for a further 24 hours, with the wire hanging from the stand, for example over the edge of a work surface.

13 Carefully attach the two vein-side-up pointed petals to the orchid, positioned just slightly behind the two side petals. Be careful not to catch the points of the petals and snap them off at this stage. Keep checking that the tape is securely fastened as you go.

10 Paint across the top of the column (once it has dried for 24 hours) with sugar glue, and position the column into the trumpet petal. Close the top of the trumpet petal over the top of the column with your fingers, lifting to adjust the closure if required.

Wiring the flower together
12 Begin to wire your flower together. Tightly wind the floral tape around the trumpet petal wire starting at the back of the flower. Wind the tape around at least twice, so it is secure. It helps to pull the tape and stretch it so that it becomes slightly stickier. One at a time, attach the two side petals to the trumpet petal by taping the wires. Do not worry if the petals are not in the exact position as they can be adjusted at the end of the taping procedure, but make sure that the tape is tight and secure — it is important to check this as you go.

14 Finally, attach the remaining vein-side-down pointed petal — this should be at the very top of the orchid, and the point should face forward. Turn the orchid around to face you, and carefully adjust the petals by manipulating them with your fingers.

Dusting the orchid
16 Dust the orchid from the center outward with pink luster powder. Tap the brush before applying it to the column and promptly disperse it over the rest of the petals. Next, dust the side petals and the pointed petals with a little light pink dust, to lift the color and make them look more natural. Keep the petals' edges a little lighter than the centers.

TIP

If you find the dusting process difficult, try coloring the petals before you wire them together.

15 Wind the floral tape down the back of the orchid wires and cut off the excess tape and wires so that there is around a 2½-inch (8 cm) stem. The orchid is now ready to be dusted with shades of pink.

Cattleya orchid
The finished orchid could be added to a spray or used alone to decorate a cake.

Sugar leaves

Leaves are an important part of a flower arrangement, although they can also look stunning in their own right — as a trail of ivy climbing a castle cake or holly leaves and a few berries on a Christmas cake. The most common leaves on cakes are ivy and rose leaves. When you are cutting out leaves, let them dry over either a piece of foam or some scrunched-up foil, so they don't end up flat and lifeless. Remember that leaves that have wire in them for flower arrangements will be inedible.

TIPS

- Leaves can look very realistic when dusted with colors, particularly fall colors. They are rarely one color only; even using different shades of green will make a leaf more lifelike.
- Some leaves are shinier than others. A shiny leaf can be achieved by simply spraying it with confectioners' glaze.

YOU WILL NEED

- White vegetable shortening
- Green gum paste
- Sugar glue (see page 172)
- Dusting colors
- Confectioners' glaze

- Rolling pin
- Rose leaf cutters
- Foam pad or foil
- Ball tool
- Green wire
- Leaf veiner
- Paintbrush

Wired rose leaf

1 Smear the work surface with white vegetable shortening, and roll out some green gum paste. As you start to roll, create a slightly thicker central ridge of gum paste, which will take the wire. Keep rolling the gum paste on either side of this ridge until it is $\frac{1}{32}$–$\frac{1}{16}$ inch (1–2 mm) thick.

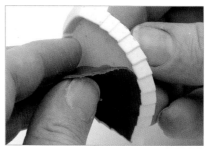

2 Place a rose leaf cutter over the top of the paste, so that the thicker ridge is running straight up the center of the leaf. Carefully peel the cutout leaf off the work surface and place it onto a foam pad or scrunched-up foil.

3 Carefully but firmly run the ball tool around the edges of the leaf, to soften them and give the leaf a more natural appearance. Keep the ball tool half on the edge of the leaf and half on the foam. Be careful not to make your leaf too frilly by going over the edges too many times — once or twice should suffice.

See also
Making sugar flowers with a veiner
134–135

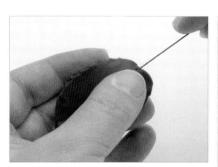

4 Cut a piece of green wire approximately 2 inches (5 cm) in length, and dip it into the sugar glue so that it coats the wire. This is essential — when the glue dries the wire will be held in place. Holding the leaf in one hand, guide the wire through the central ridge you created in step 1. As the wire moves through the ridge, hold two fingers either side of the ridge to keep the wire from escaping through the gum paste.

6 Gently remove the leaf from the veiner and place it on the foam pad or crumpled foil to dry. Let it dry overnight at room temperature.

7 Dusting or spraying the leaves with color adds a new dimension to the finished product. Rose leaves dusted with different shades of green will appear more realistic. If you are able to get a real rose leaf, use it as reference. If you like, spray your leaf with confectioners' glaze for a shiny finish. Make sure that you either spray the leaf outdoors, or onto a piece of paper towel in a well-ventilated room.

5 Push the wire slowly until it is approximately halfway through the leaf. Place the leaf onto the veiner, lining up the center of the leaf. Then press the other side of the veiner onto the leaf and push down quite hard. This procedure will emboss the leaf on both sides.

Sugar leaves
A selection of sugar leaves, with their wires left long for attaching to a cake.

CHAPTER 8

Chocolate

The use of chocolate in cake decoration has increased
in popularity substantially over the past few years. The aim
of this chapter is to provide you with the basic skills to
work confidently with chocolate and create some
beautiful decorations.

Equipment for working with chocolate

The equipment listed on these pages will help you to begin to work confidently with chocolate in a variety of ways: from tempering chocolate at home to using chocolate paste to create fantastic decorations.

Spatula

It is important to create a uniform temperature while tempering chocolate so a spatula is a must for vigorous stirring.

Metal cutters

As with sugar in the previous chapter, you can use cutters to make some really impressive flowers from chocolate paste.

Pan and glass bowl

To temper chocolate using the seeding method you will need a glass bowl and a saucepan to melt the chocolate.

Large palette knife

This kitchen basic is the best tool to use for spreading chocolate, and can also be used to check the success of chocolate tempering.

Chocolate thermometer

Although by no means essential, this may prove a useful piece of equipment when tempering chocolate.

Microwave

The quickest and easiest way to temper chocolate at home is to buy pre-tempered chocolate and melt it in the microwave.

Transfer sheers
Above and below: *These acetate sheets are available in a huge range of colors and patterns so you can choose one that really reflects the theme of your cake.*

Plastic bowls
If you are tempering chocolate in the microwave it is essential that you use a plastic bowl, not a glass one.

Textured rolling pin
You can easily create an interesting texture on your chocolate paste to give a softer appearance to chocolate fans.

Plastic side scraper
A plastic side scraper is a great tool to use for cutting rolled chocolate paste as it will not drag the chocolate.

Acetate sheets
Chocolate paste melts easily and can be very sticky so you may find it helpful to have some acetate sheets on hand to press the chocolate between for shaping.

Tempering chocolate

Good-quality chocolate contains cocoa butter crystals. Tempering chocolate is a process where the chocolate is heated to a controlled temperature so that these crystals become uniform. Tempered chocolate sets very hard. When it is broken it snaps rather than bends, and it has a shiny appearance as opposed to a dull one (which may even contain a slightly streaky or white "bloom" effect). Chocolate that has been tempered correctly will release easily from molds.

YOU WILL NEED

- Couverture chocolate buttons

- Plastic bowl
- Plastic spatula
- Saucepan
- Glass bowl
- Chocolate thermometer (optional)
- Palette knife or spoon

Types of chocolate

There are two types of chocolate available to purchase: couverture and confectionery coating chocolate. Couverture chocolate usually contains a minimum of 32 percent cocoa butter, while coating chocolate has little or no cocoa butter. Therefore, couverture has a far superior taste to coating chocolate, but it will require tempering before it can be used. Dark chocolate has the most cocoa butter in it.

There are many ways to temper chocolate, some including the use of a marble slab to cool the chocolate to the correct temperature. The easiest, cleanest and quickest way to temper chocolate for the home cake decorator is to buy pre-tempered couverture buttons or "callets" and melt these slowly in the microwave. Callets are available from most cake decorating stores. An alternative method is known

as "seeding," and this too is relatively straightforward, doesn't require any specialized equipment and doesn't require a microwave.

Alternatively, there are many "tempering machines" available to buy, and if you are planning to make many chocolate cake decorations this may be a worthwhile investment.

TIP

Important: Confectionery coating chocolate and couverture chocolate should never be mixed. They cannot be used together, even in painting details.

Microwave method
1 Place the couverture chocolate buttons in a plastic bowl. The bowl must be plastic — glass retains heat and will interfere with the control of the heating process; the chocolate will soon become too hot and will not temper correctly.

See also
Using molds with chocolate **74–77**
Chocolate transfer sheets **158–161**

2 Heat the chocolate on full power for 10 seconds, and then remove the bowl from the microwave and stir. Place the bowl back in the microwave and repeat this process. Do not be tempted to increase the time, as microwaves form "hot spots" and the chocolate will become too warm in places and will not temper correctly.

3 Keep melting and stirring until the chocolate starts to turn to liquid. Once the buttons have almost melted, stop heating and continue to stir vigorously, making sure that you scrape the sides of the bowl with your spatula to incorporate all of the chocolate and create an even temperature. This completes the tempering process.

Seeding method
1 Melt two-thirds of the couverture chocolate buttons to 113°F (45°C) in a glass bowl over a pan of boiling water. Be extremely careful not to burn yourself. Make sure that no water or steam comes into contact with the chocolate you are melting, otherwise it will be instantly ruined.

2 Remove the chocolate from the heat, and pour it into a plastic bowl containing the remaining (unmelted) third of your chocolate buttons. Stir the chocolate well — the unmelted buttons will bring the heat of the chocolate down as they melt. Keep stirring until they are all melted. This completes the tempering process.

TIPS

To test whether your chocolate is correctly tempered, dip a clean palette knife or the back of a metal spoon into the chocolate. Let it set for two to three minutes. If the chocolate sets, has a shiny finish and snaps easily, it is correctly tempered and is ready to use.

While a chocolate thermometer is not a necessity, if you do want to check the temperature of your chocolate for some additional reassurance, note that the tempering temperature is slightly different for each type of chocolate. Couverture dark chocolate is correctly tempered at 89°F (31°C), couverture milk chocolate at 86°F (30°C) and couverture white chocolate at 84°F (29°C).

Chocolate transfer sheets

Chocolate transfer sheets are acetate sheets that have a pattern on them made of cocoa butter. Cocoa butter, in its original form, is a pale yellow color and is essentially the fat content of a cocoa bean. Additional food colors can be added to the cocoa butter. If you pour tempered chocolate onto a transfer sheet, when it sets, the pattern from the transfer sheet will be imprinted on it. Transfer sheets are available in a huge range of patterns and colors, including stripes, checks, musical notes and animal prints. They can create all kinds of exciting effects.

YOU WILL NEED

- Small cake — 2-inch (5 cm) diameter x 1½-inch (4 cm) height prepared with buttercream and covered in chocolate paste
- Transfer sheets
- Couverture dark chocolate (tempered)
- Sugar blossom

- Tape measure
- Scissors
- Large palette knife
- Sharp knife
- Assortment of metal cutters

TIP

When preparing your cake, apply a light coating of buttercream and cover it with chocolate paste using the method as described on pages 32–33. Don't worry if the finish on the cake isn't perfect — once the transfer sheet is on it will all be covered. The chocolate paste is simply there as a seal between the cake and the chocolate, to increase the shelf life of your finished cake and so the chocolate transfer sheet has a surface to stick to.

Individual wrapped cake
1 Calculate the circumference of your cake and add an additional ½ inch (1.5 cm) to this measurement to create an overlap. The transfer sheet should be 2 inches (5 cm) in height so it is slightly higher than the cake itself.

2 Cut out the transfer sheet carefully. Try to avoid touching the pattern on the transfer sheet, as the heat from your hands will melt it.

See also
Transfer sheets on fondant **110–111**
Tempering chocolate **156–157**

3 Temper some dark chocolate as described on pages 156–157. Lay the transfer sheet onto the work surface pattern side up and, with a palette knife, spread the chocolate onto the sheet. Coat the transfer sheet to approximately ⅛ inch (2–3 mm) thick.

5 Overlap the ends of the transfer sheet and let the chocolate dry for 20–30 minutes at room temperature. Don't be tempted to spend time adjusting the sheet — once it is in position, allow it to set.

6 Carefully peel away the transfer sheet to reveal the pattern. When the sheet is peeled away, the join in the set chocolate will barely be noticeable.

Completed mini cake
Pipe a swirl of chocolate fudge icing into the middle of the cake and add a sugar blossom.

4 Pick up the coated transfer sheet and wrap it around your prepared cake as quickly as you can (see tip on facing page). Wrap the sheet toward you, as this makes it easier to see what you are doing. Try to hold the ends of the sheet only, otherwise your fingers will remove the chocolate.

Colorful chocolate
White or colored chocolate decorations can add a splash of color to your cakes and will contrast with milk or dark chocolate.

Transfer shards

1 Temper some chocolate (see pages 156–157), and spread it onto the transfer sheet, around ⅛ inch (2–3 mm) thick. At this stage the chocolate will appear shiny. If the chocolate has been correctly tempered it will start to turn dull, setting from the outside to the center, within 3–4 minutes.

2 When all of the chocolate has gone dull but not set completely, use a sharp knife to cut out a variety of different-sized shards. Work quickly as the chocolate will continue to set. (If you are cutting out shapes with a cutter, it may be easier to cut in smaller batches as the chocolate can set very quickly and become difficult to cut.)

3 Once you have cut out all of your shapes, let the chocolate set for a further 20–30 minutes in the refrigerator to allow the pattern to transfer completely before peeling off the transfer sheet. Remove the chocolate from the fridge and do not store the chocolate in there once it has set.

TIP

Transfer sheets can also be cut into other shapes — hearts for example, or shards. There are so many patterns to choose from, suitable for any occasion. Always take note of the pattern on the transfer sheet before deciding which chocolate — milk, white or dark — to use. For example, a transfer sheet with a white pattern will not show up particularly well on white chocolate but will look dramatic on dark or milk chocolate.

Unique design
Attach the shards to a cake with some buttercream that has a small amount of chocolate added to it — approximately one-third melted chocolate to two-thirds buttercream, plus 1 to 2 tablespoons (15–30 ml) of water if the mixture is very stiff once the chocolate begins to set.

Chocolate fans

Chocolate fans are a very simple but effective way of adding additional decoration to a chocolate cake. They can be made from white, milk, dark or colored chocolate pastes and in a variety of sizes, and they may be either plain or detailed by using a textured rolling pin. You can even give them a shiny finish by spraying them with confectioners' glaze. By making the fans a few hours in advance of completing your cake, they will have set and will hold their shape beautifully. They can be made up to a month in advance and stored in cool, dry, dark conditions.

TIP

Knead the chocolate paste on confectioners' sugar. Be careful not to over-knead the paste, as it will become sticky with the warmth of your hands.

YOU WILL NEED

- Chocolate paste
- Confectioners' sugar

- Rolling pin
- Textured rolling pin (optional)
- Plastic side scraper

1 Roll out the chocolate paste into a strip approximately ⅛ inch (2–3 mm) thick. Different lengths and widths of chocolate paste strips will create different styles of fans.

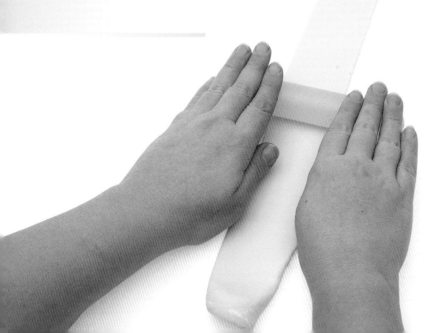

2 Either leave the fan plain or roll with a textured rolling pin at this stage.

3 Cut out the strips of paste with a plastic side scraper. These work well with chocolate paste as they don't tend to drag it.

See also
Making a fondant ribbon rose
136–137

4 Carefully pick up the strip of paste and hold it in your left hand. Begin to pleat the paste with your right hand (or the other way around, if you are left-handed), folding each pleat carefully as you go. Make sure your thumb doesn't move up the side of the pleat; this could result in the pleats becoming squashed.

6 Pinch the bottom of the fan together to tighten the pleats and secure it.

7 Cut off the excess paste with the plastic side scraper. Let the fan dry for 2–3 hours. Once the chocolate starts to set again, the fan will hold its shape.

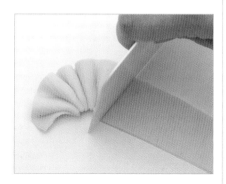

5 Once you have pleated the whole strip, place the fan on your work surface and cut off the excess with the plastic side scraper.

Completed fans
Choose white, milk, dark or colored chocolate paste to best complement your design. Attach the completed fans to your cake with a little chocolate buttercream or some tempered chocolate.

Chocolate roses

Chocolate roses of milk, white or dark chocolate paste are quick and easy to make with a little practice. Once you have mastered them, you will find this skill valuable in creating all kinds of cakes. They can be made up to a month in advance, if stored correctly in a cool, dry, dark place away from strong odors. Don't be tempted to store them in the refrigerator though, where they will suffer from the effects of condensation.

White chocolate roses finished with pink luster spray.

YOU WILL NEED

- Chocolate paste
- Confectioners' sugar
- Dusting colors and sprays (optional)

- Petal-shaped cutters
- Rolling pin
- Acetate sheets (optional)
- Plastic side scraper
- Star-shaped metal cutters (optional)
- Paintbrush (optional)

TIP

Chocolate paste will stick to itself, so there is no need to use any further liquid or sugar glue (see page 172) to assemble the rose. There is a fine balance to correctly rolling out chocolate paste. Try to have a film of confectioners' sugar on your work surface — no more. If there is too much, the petals will be too dry and will not stick to each other, and if you don't have enough, the chocolate paste is likely to stick to you!

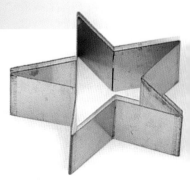

Milk chocolate roses

See also
Using cutters **82–83**
Wired sugar rose **138–142**

Rosebud

1 Form a ball of chocolate paste by rolling the paste in confectioners' sugar at first and then in your hand. Continue to roll just one half of the ball so it narrows to form the correct cone shape. Don't spend too long forming the cone — the more you roll the paste, the stickier it will become with the heat from your hands.

2 Check that the cone is the correct size for the rose by holding it against the cutter — from the base of the cutter to the tip of the cone, it should be able to fit. (It is easiest to learn this technique with a medium-sized petal cutter.) Place the cone flat on its bottom on your work surface.

3 Roll out some more chocolate paste onto a small amount of confectioners' sugar. Compared to gum paste, chocolate paste needs to be rolled out much thicker, around ⅛ inch (4 mm). Cut out some rose petals; you will need 11 petals for a large rose, six for a medium rose and three for a rosebud.

4 Gently pinch the edges of each petal to soften their appearance — if you don't do this the rose will look lifeless. This can be done either directly with your fingers, or you can put the petals between two sheets of clear acetate and press the edges that way. If you suffer from hot hands, you may find it easier to use acetate sheets.

5 Wrap the first petal around the cone, with the point of the petal facing downward so that it overlaps and the center of the cone is completely covered.

6 Position the next two petals opposite each other and in line around the center petal, and interlink them as shown. Try not to hold onto the petals for too long, as they will start to melt in your hands!

Continued on next page ▶

7 Gently bend the petals backward to give the rose effect. At the end of this stage you have formed a rosebud.

Full rose

8 Attach the next three petals by pressing the side of each petal into the chocolate paste at the bottom of the rose. Ensure each is attached, then begin overlapping each one around the cone, making sure they are in line with the top of the cone. At this stage the rose is just starting to open out.

9 Once the petals are attached as before, you can gently bend the petals back. It is better, if you are making a spray of roses, to have roses at three different stages, as this gives a more natural effect.

10 For a full rose, attach the remaining five petals. If, at this stage, the outer petals are struggling to stay in place, pick up the cone, tip it upside down, and gently rub the joins of the paste with your forefinger so that the petals stick to the cone. By rubbing the rose with your finger you will heat up the paste and it will weld together. Gently bend back the petals again to form the final rose.

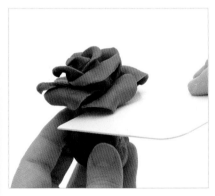

11 Remove the completed rose — be it at bud, halfway or full stage — by sliding a plastic side scraper under the rose and cutting it away from the excess paste left on the cone. Let it dry for several hours at room temperature, away from direct sunlight.

13 If you would like a colored effect on your roses, then you can either lightly dust the edges with some dusting colors or spray them. Dark and milk chocolate roses look fantastic when parts of the petals are dusted with gold edible dusting color, especially as part of Christmas-style designs. Likewise, a white chocolate rose sprayed with a pearl spray adds a touch of elegance. Chocolate roses also look glamorous when they are sprinkled with edible glitters.

12 A calyx can be added, but is not essential, by cutting out a star shape of chocolate paste in the same color as your rose — or you might like to color some white chocolate green, by dusting the calyx before attaching it. Paint a small amount of water directly onto the underside of the calyx to get it to stick to the bottom of the rose.

Individual treat
Mini chocolate cake with a chocolate rose and fan.

Recipes

The recipes included in this section have been used throughout the book. They will allow you to create delicious cakes, coverings and fillings that will provide you with a good base for your decorating.

CHOCOLATE CAKE

For quantities and ingredients, see table below.

1 Preheat the oven to 330°F (165°C).

2 Line the sides and the base of the cake pan with parchment paper.

3 With a hand-held or stand mixer, cream the butter and sugar together in a bowl.

4 Add the eggs one at a time, along with 1 tablespoon (15 ml) of self-rising flour.

5 Sift the remaining flour and cocoa powder into the mixture and carefully fold it in with a metal spoon.

6 Spoon the mixture into the pan and bake in the center of the oven according to the cooking time shown in the table below.

7 Test the cake to check that it is fully cooked by inserting a skewer into the middle. If the skewer comes out clean, the cake is ready.

8 Remove the cake from the oven, and leave it to cool in its pan for a few minutes before carefully placing it on a cooling rack.

TIP

There are some pre-mixed sponge cake mixes available on the market. These usually just require adding oil, water, and eggs.

SPONGE CAKE

This is the same as the chocolate cake but without the cocoa powder. Replace the cocoa powder with the same amount of self-rising flour.

LEMON CAKE

This is the same as the chocolate cake but without the cocoa powder. Instead, replace the cocoa powder with the same amount of self-rising flour and add the grated zest and juice of a lemon.

NUMBER OF PORTIONS

Based on a 2 x 1 in. (5 x 2.5 cm) slice

Size of cake	Round sponge	Square sponge
4 in. (10 cm)	10	14
6 in. (15 cm)	14	18
8 in. (20 cm)	25	32
10 in. (25 cm)	39	50

QUANTITIES AND INGREDIENTS FOR CHOCOLATE CAKE

Size of cake	Butter	Superfine sugar	Eggs (medium)	Cocoa powder	Self-rising flour	Cooking time
4 in. (10 cm)	7 tbsp (105 ml)	½ cup (125 ml)	2	3½ tbsp (52 ml)	1 cup (250 ml)	1 hour
6 in. (15 cm)	¾ cup (175 ml)	1 cup (250 ml)	3	3½ tbsp (52 ml)	1½ cups (375 ml)	1¼ hours
8 in. (20 cm)	1¾ cups (425 ml)	2²/₃ cups (575 ml)	7	¹/₃ cup (75 ml)	4 cups (1 L)	1¾ hours
10 in. (25 cm)	2²/₃ cups (650 ml)	3¼ cups (810 ml)	10	½ cup (125 ml)	5²/₃ cups (1.4 L)	2–2½ hours

See also
Designing cakes: Avoiding waste **12**
Royal icing **50–51**

CUPCAKES

For 12 muffin-sized cupcakes:
- 1¼ cups (310 ml) superfine sugar
- 1 cup (250 ml) butter
- 2 cups (500 ml) self-rising flour
- 4 large eggs
- 1 tsp (5 ml) baking soda
- 12 cupcake liners
- 12-hole muffin pan

1 Preheat the oven to 360°F (180°C). Place the cupcake liners into a muffin pan.
2 Beat the sugar and butter together for a couple of minutes in a food processor or with a whisk.
3 Add the eggs one at a time, adding a spoonful of flour each time.
4 Sift in the remaining flour and baking soda, slowly incorporating them into the mixture with a metal spoon or in the food processor on a slow pulse setting.
5 Fill the cupcake liners approximately two-thirds full.
6 Bake in the oven for around 20 minutes or until the tops of the cakes spring back when you touch them.
7 Let the cupcakes cool on a wire rack prior to decoration.
8 Cupcakes can be stored in the freezer for up to a month.

BUTTERCREAM

This recipe will produce a creamy yellow mixture.

- 7¾ cups (1.9 L) confectioners' sugar
- 2¼ cups (560 ml) butter, room temperature
- 1 tbsp (15 ml) water

1 Put the confectioners' sugar and butter in a bowl, add the water and begin to mix them together at a low speed. Do not start the mixer on a high speed, otherwise the confectioners' sugar will end up everywhere.
2 If you want to really soften the mixture, and use it to pipe onto cupcakes for example, prepare it in a food processor. Once the initial confectioners' sugar is incorporated, turn up the speed and let the machine really beat the mixture for two to three minutes, until it is very soft and light.
3 Buttercream can be stored in the refrigerator for up to three weeks. Keep it in a bowl and covered with plastic wrap on the surface of the buttercream and then another layer of plastic wrap across the top of the bowl, to keep it airtight. This keeps the buttercream from drying out.

ALTERNATIVE BUTTERCREAM

This recipe will produce a white-colored buttercream.

- ²⁄₃ cup (150 ml) plus 3 tbsp (45 ml) water
- 1 oz. (28 g) meringue powder
- 10 cups (2.5 L) sifted confectioners' sugar
- 3½ tsp (17 ml) white vegetable shortening
- 3 tbsp (45 ml) glycerine
- ¾ tsp (3 ml) salt
- ¾ tsp (3 ml) clear almond extract
- ¾ tsp (3 ml) clear vanilla extract
- ¾ tsp (3 ml) butter flavor (no color)

1 Mix the water with the meringue powder with an electric beater until it begins to form peaks.
2 Add the confectioners' sugar 1 cup (250 ml) at a time, keeping the speed of the mixer slow to keep it from going everywhere.
3 Add the remaining 3 tbsp (45 ml) of water, the white vegetable shortening and the glycerine and then mix well.
4 Finally, add the salt and the flavorings, and keep mixing until the buttercream is smooth.
5 To alter the consistency of the buttercream, simply add water and mix, but be careful not to add too much.

CHOCOLATE BUTTERCREAM

For chocolate cupcakes or a chocolate filling, add melted chocolate to your buttercream recipes — usually approximately two-thirds buttercream to one-third melted chocolate. Add a few tablespoons of water if the mixture starts to set. Flavor the buttercream with peppermint and dark chocolate, orange oil and milk chocolate, or lemon and white chocolate for interesting taste variations.

CHOCOLATE FUDGE ICING

- ⅔ cup (150 ml) butter
- ¼ cup (60 ml) cocoa powder
- 1 cup (250 ml) confectioners' sugar
- 3 tbsp (45 ml) milk

1 Melt the butter in a pan over a gentle heat, then increase the heat slightly and add the cocoa powder. Mix well.
2 Add the confectioners' sugar to the mixture and keep stirring.
3 Finally, add the milk. Keep stirring until the mixture becomes a glossy, smooth paste.

CHOCOLATE GANACHE

- ¾ cup (175 ml) whipping cream
- 2 tbsp (30 ml) butter
- 7 oz. (200 g) dark chocolate buttons

1 Heat the cream and butter and pour the mixture over the dark chocolate buttons.
2 Stir the mixture until smooth. The basic mixture can be enhanced with the addition of alcohol or flavoring extracts.

Once made, ganache will keep in the fridge in an airtight container for approximately two weeks. The addition of any alcohol will extend the shelf life to four weeks.

RICH FRUIT CAKE

For quantities and ingredients, see table at right.
1 Preheat the oven to 360°F (180°C).
2 With a hand-held or stand mixer, cream the butter and brown sugar together, and then gradually add the eggs one at a time, with 1 tablespoon (15 ml) of all-purpose flour each time.
3 Sift in the remaining flour, and mix carefully with a metal spoon or on a slow pulse in a food processor.
4 Add the dried fruit and the remaining ingredients, mix well and pour into a cake pan lined with parchment paper.
5 Place on the middle rack of the oven (for cooking time, see table at right).
6 Near the end of the time, check to see if the cake is cooked by placing a clean skewer into the center of the cake; if it comes out clean, the cake is ready.
7 Let it cool completely before decorating.

TIP
It is possible to purchase ready-made fillings from grocery stores and cake decorating suppliers if you are short on time or prefer not to make your own.

See also
Covering a cake with marzipan **30–31**
Recipes: Marzipan **172**

QUANTITIES AND INGREDIENTS FOR RICH FRUIT CAKE

Ingredients	Size of cake		
	6 in. (15 cm) round or 5 in. (13 cm) square	8 in. (20 cm) round or 7 in. (18 cm) square	10 in. (25 cm) round or 9 in. (23 cm) square
Currants	¾ cup (175 ml)	1¾ cups (425 ml)	3⅓ cups (825 ml)
Raisins	½ cup (125 ml)	1¼ cups (310 ml)	2¼ cups (560 ml)
Golden raisins	½ cup (125 ml)	1¼ cups (310 ml)	2¼ cups (560 ml)
Mixed peel	1 oz. (30 g)	2 oz. (60 g)	4 oz. (110 g)
Candied cherries	1½ oz. (40 g)	3 oz. (80 g)	5 oz. (140 g)
Ground almonds	⅓ cup (75 ml)	⅔ cup (150 ml)	1¼ cups (310 ml)
Lemon rind	½ lemon	¾ lemon	1 lemon
All-purpose flour	¾ cup (175 ml)	1⅔ cups (400 ml)	3 cups (750 ml)
Cinnamon	½ tsp (2 ml)	¾ tsp (3 ml)	½ tbsp (7 ml)
Pumpkin pie spice	¼ tsp (1 ml)	½ tsp (2 ml)	1 tsp (5 ml)
Butter	6 tbsp (90 ml)	¾ cup (175 ml)	1½ cups (375 ml)
Soft brown sugar	⅓ cup (75 ml)	⅔ cup (150 ml)	1⅔ cups (400 ml)
Eggs (medium)	2	3	6
Molasses	1 tsp (5 ml)	1 tbsp (15 ml)	1 tbsp (15 ml)

COOKING TIMES FOR RICH FRUIT CAKE

Size of cake	Cooking time
6 in. (15 cm) round or 5 in. (13 cm) square	2 hours
8 in. (20 cm) round or 7 in. (18 cm) square	2¾ hours
6 in. (15 cm) round or 5 in. (13 cm) square	3¾ hours

MARZIPAN

- 1 cup (250 ml) golden superfine sugar
- 2 cups (500 ml) confectioners' sugar, sifted, plus extra for dusting
- 1 lb. (450 g) ground almonds
- Flavoring, such as the seeds from a vanilla bean or 2 tsp (10 ml) rum (if using rum, a little extra confectioners' sugar is required).
- 2 eggs, beaten

1 Place the sugars and ground almonds in a large bowl.
2 Rub in the vanilla seeds or add the rum.
3 Make a well in the middle of the mixture, add the eggs and blend using a knife.
4 Dust the work surface with confectioners' sugar and knead the marzipan to a smooth dough. Don't overdo the kneading, since this will make the marzipan greasy. Add more confectioners' sugar if the paste becomes too sticky.

SUGAR GLUE

- ½ tsp (2 ml) gum tragacanth
- 3 tbsp (45 ml) warm boiled water

1 Sprinkle the gum tragacanth powder over the warm water and mix.
2 Leave until the powder is absorbed, and then mix again. The mixture should be clear. The glue will be smooth, without lumps, and have a soft consistency. If the glue thickens or is too thick for your needs, add a little more warm water.

FONDANT

Using store-bought fondant, which is available from specialty stores, saves time and the consistency is constant and much less likely to crack and dry. If you prefer to make your own, or have difficulty finding fondant, this recipe makes 4½ lb. (2 kg).

- 2 packets (2½ tbsp/37 ml) gelatin
- ½ cup (125 ml) cold water
- 2 tbsp (30 ml) glycerol
- 1 cup (250 ml) liquid glucose
- 4½ lb. (2 kg) confectioners' sugar, plus extra for dusting

1 Sprinkle the gelatin over the cold water in a bowl and let it soak until it is spongy.
2 Stand the bowl over boiled water and stir until the gelatin dissolves.
3 Stir in the glycerol and glucose.
4 Sift the confectioners' sugar into a bowl and make a well in the center.
5 Slowly pour in the liquid, constantly stirring. Mix well.
6 Pour the fondant onto a work surface that has been well dusted with confectioners' sugar, and knead until smooth.

Tips for baking

A few basic rules apply to baking, which, when observed, remove many of the uncertainties and help to avoid possible mistakes.

- Always read the recipe through from start to finish before you begin. Then, make sure that all of the ingredients are available. If you do not have all the ingredients on hand, do not try to substitute or adjust any of the quantities; choose another recipe instead.
- Ensure all equipment for making and baking is grease-free.
- Assemble all the ingredients, and, if possible, leave them in the kitchen for around an hour so they can all reach the same temperature. Everything should be ready to go when you begin baking.
- Always measure accurately, using only one set of measurements. Never switch between imperial and metric.
- Always grease and line cake pans correctly; it saves so much frustration later.
- Heat the oven for 20 minutes before the cake goes in to ensure that the temperature will be constant from the start. An accurate oven is essential for successful baking; a discrepancy of a few degrees in the temperature can have a disastrous effect. Regular checking with an oven thermometer helps avoid this.
- Place the cake in the center of the oven, not touching the sides. Never open the oven door until at least three-quarters of the cooking time has elapsed, otherwise the delicate structure may collapse.

WHAT WENT WRONG?

Cake sinks in the center

This is usually because the cake isn't cooked in the middle. Test the cake by inserting a skewer into the deepest part. If it comes out clean it is cooked; if not, cook for a little longer. Sometimes overbeating the cake at the batter stage can over-aerate it, which will cause it to sink during or shortly after baking. Always make sure you follow the cake proportions correctly.

Domed/cracked top

This isn't really a problem since the cake can simply be leveled. However, if you make the center of the cake slightly lower than the edges when you fill the cake pan, the cooked cake will have balanced out. The top cracks because the outside of the cake has cooked more quickly than the center, and the center then cooks and expands, cracking the top. A slightly cooler oven will allow the cake to cook at a more even rate.

Grainy appearance and dry cake

The cake was not mixed sufficiently and may have also contained insufficient liquid. Milk can always be added if the mixture looks too dry.

Cake is burned

The cake was left too long in the oven, or the oven is heating incorrectly. You may be able to resurrect the cake by cutting away the burned section, but take care that the flavor of the rest of the cake isn't affected.

Cake is too heavy/dense

This is usually due to too much flour or to overmixing the flour, so take care not to measure your ingredients using two different measuring systems. The oven could also be too hot, so if this is a recurring problem, an oven thermometer might be a worthwhile purchase.

- A cooked cake should have risen well, be slightly domed in the middle and have a golden color; it should be shrinking ever so slightly from the sides of the pan.
- To test if the cake is ready, lightly press a finger on the center of the cake, which should feel firm and springy. If an impression of your finger remains, bake for a few minutes more. Insert a skewer into the center of the cake and withdraw it slowly. It should come out clean; if any cake mix sticks, cook for a little longer.

Index

Author acknowledgments

This book is dedicated to my mother Susan, my inspiration. I'd like to thank firstly my family, Chris, Charlotte and Kelly, who put up famously with my creative ways: Chris for his patience and understanding, all 18 plus years of it, Charlotte for her sense of humor and love of shopping, and Kelly for our joint love of all things leopard print — the duck cupcakes are just for you. Thanks to my wonderful team at Tracey's Cakes, who do a fantastic job, Alice Fonda Marsland, my NEC partner in crime and Carol Stoodley, I've never been so organized; Sue and Mike Gough, Evira and Tony Rosewell, Jenny Mann, Donna Wells, Londer Gray, my very good friends, thank goodness for them; all the wonderful ladies at A Piece of Cake in Thame, the central hub of my cake decorating life, specifically Norma, who can sell me anything, and Jenny for her assistance with the sugar rose; I'm dedicating my flipflop cupcake to Heather, and thank you to Angela my toughest, but fairest, critic. Final thank you to Quarto for asking me in the first place to write about a subject I'm so passionate about.

A note on terminology

Cake decorating terminology can be confusing and difficult to grasp. As you begin to explore the world of cake decorating, you will come to realize that many terms are used interchangeably — by beginners and experts alike. For clarity and consistency, we have used the following terminology in this book:

Fondant: a soft, sweet icing that can be rolled out to cover cakes before adding further decorations. It is ideal for use with molds, cutters, sugar-craft guns and bead makers. When modeling, add a little gum tragacanth to your fondant to add elasticity and help it set and you can create beautiful, stable, edible creations.

Gum paste: a malleable and elastic paste which can be rolled very thin, making it perfect for creating delicate decorations and realistic looking sugar flowers which can be stored for long periods of time. Although nontoxic, your creations will dry very hard and will not usually be consumed.

Suppliers

Tracey's Cakes
5 Wheelwright Road
Longwick
Princes Risborough
Bucks, HP27 9ST
UK
Tel: +44 01844 347147
www.traceyscakes.co.uk

PME Arts and Crafts Ltd
USA Distribution Center
518 Middle Avenue
Aurora, IL 60506
Tel: 630-859-3989
www.pmeartsandcrafts.com

Wilton Industries
2240 west 75th Street
Woodbridge, IL 60517
Tel: 800-794-5866
www.wilton.com

**Cake Decorators School
and Supplies**
244 Hall Avenue
Meriden, CT 06450
Tel: 203-634-1716
www.cakedecorators.com

Cake Carousel
1002 N. Central Expressway
Suite 501
Richardson, TX 75080
Tel: 972-690-4628 or
877-814-6670
www.cakecarousel.com

Confectionately Yours
4160 Market Street, Unit 9
Ventura, CA 93003
Tel: 805-850-0400
www.confectionatelyyours.net

Michaels Stores Inc.
8000 Bent Branch Drive
Irving, TX 75063
Tel: 1-800-642-4235
www.michaels.com

Sugarcraft, Inc.
3665 Dixie Highway
Hamilton, OH 45015
Tel: 513-896-7089
www.sugarcraft.com